John Kirkwood

An autumn Holiday in the United States and Canada

John Kirkwood

An autumn Holiday in the United States and Canada

ISBN/EAN: 9783337189648

Printed in Europe, USA, Canada, Australia, Japan

Cover: Foto ©Andreas Hilbeck / pixelio.de

More available books at **www.hansebooks.com**

AN

AUTUMN HOLIDAY

IN THE

UNITED STATES AND CANADA.

BY THE
REV. JOHN KIRKWOOD,
TROON.

Edinburgh:
ANDREW ELLIOT, 11 Princes Street.

MDCCCLXXXVII.

PREFACE.

To those who seek to spend a holiday beyond our own shores, the Continent of Europe has hitherto had the chief attractions. Its Norwegian Fiords, its glorious Alps, its ancient cities, and the calm retreats on the blue Mediterranean, are deserved favourites. But the American Continent has claims peculiarly its own. It is not without its grand and varied scenery; and its history, if modern, is marvellous, not in the records and wars of princes, but in the signs of the progress of a great people. It has, indeed, here and there, footprints of the past—marks of earnest and successful struggles for liberty—but the present sons of the soil are constantly achieving conquests by the ploughshare, the mining pick, and the mechanic's hammer, whose traces may be found everywhere. They are famous for valuable discoveries and inventions, and important schemes for social and religious advancement. They are already rich in the memory of illustrious men, and have among the living many of the excellent of the earth. The colonization of their vast territories excels, in extent and romantic interest, any in the history of the world. The immigrants are from all nations, yet the prevailing influence and welding power are those of our own race, language, and religion. In their institutions we may see the fruits—often the riper fruits—of our own earlier civilization. In the great body of the people we find proofs of genuine regard for the mother country, which we ought cordially to reciprocate, not looking with jealousy, but with pride, on the progress and attainments of our kith and kin. And among them we may discover friends of former days, or be introduced to those, hitherto strangers, who give us the warmest of welcomes.

The dreaded Atlantic, which lies between, is the great barrier in the way of many. But if it has its drawbacks, it has also its advantages. If it sometimes destroys our physical comfort and equilibrium, it brings complete isolation and rest from the cares of the outer world, and is, generally, in the highest degree, health-giving. Every convenience, and even luxury, may be enjoyed in crossing; the time occupied furnishes a sufficient specimen of an ocean voyage without its tedium; while the facilities for speedy and comfortable travelling are, on the other side, unsurpassed.

Surely all this may well lend a charm to a holiday in America not exceeded by any European one, and give to the record of it a special interest to readers at home. The field is familiar to many; and not a few who have gone there have brought back their sheaves with them. But abundant gleanings are always left, and each visitor may gather and bring back something more, if not something altogether new, which may be scattered, perhaps on fresh and receptive soil, as a return for the seeds our sons originally received from ourselves. At all events, it was with this hope that I was induced to write a series of papers in the *Ardrossan and Saltcoats Herald*, on my recent tour in the United States and Canada, and have again been persuaded to reproduce them in a more permanent, and, I trust, a more improved form in the following pages.

CONTENTS.

CHAPTER I.

THE VOYAGE.—Stormy Prospect—Ireland's Industry and Mail Claims—Smooth Seas and Lively Decks—Sights and Sounds—Banks of Newfoundland—Remains of the Oregon—Last Sunset at Sea—The New World. *Pp. 9-20.*

CHAPTER II.

NEW YORK AND ITS CHURCHES.—Sabbath Entrance—The Gates of the City—The View—The Welcome—Broadway Tabernacle—Fifth Avenue Presbyterian Church—The Christian Brethren—Coloured Congregation—Zeal of the Churches. *Pp. 21-33.*

CHAPTER III.

NEW YORK SCHOOLS.—Specimen of Public Day-school—Attendance—Punishment—Value of System—Sabbath Schools—Young Men's Christian Association. *Pp. 34-43.*

CHAPTER IV.

NEW YORK—WORK AND WAYS.—Harper's Printing Establishment—Hotels—Arrangement of Streets—Broadway and its Business—Fifth Avenue—Elevated Railroad—Battery-park—Central-park—Grave of General Grant. *Pp. 44-56.*

CHAPTER V.

SHORT EXCURSIONS.—Coney Island—Colossal Elephant—Colossal Advertisements—Brooklyn: its Churches, its Park, its Bridge—The Hudson—West Point. *Pp. 57-68.*

CHAPTER VI.

TO THE CITY OF PENN.—Newark—Orange—Princeton—Philadelphia. *Pp. 69-85.*

CHAPTER VII.

TO NIAGARA.—The Katskill Mountains—Railway Kitchen and other conveniences and inconveniences—Mohawk Valley—Origin of Mormonism—Buffalo—Froude and the Falls—Niagara River—Niagara Village—Clearances—The Scene. *Pp. 86-100.*

CHAPTER VIII.

TO MONTREAL.—Galt—Hamilton—Ontario—Toronto—The St. Lawrence—Thousand Islands—Victoria Bridge—The Ice Bridge—Canadian Cottage—The Mountain. *Pp. 101-118.*

CONTENTS.

CHAPTER IX.

TO QUEBEC.—Lachine Rapids—Indians—Night on the St. Lawrence—Morning glory—Point Levi—Cape Diamond—Chamber of Representatives—Plains of Abraham—Wolfe's Cove—Old Town—French Canadians. *Pp.* 119-138.

CHAPTER X.

TO BOSTON.—Sabbath at Montreal—Back Woods—Lake Champlain—Albany Capitol and Park—Springfield—Boston—Bunker's Hill—Harvard University—Poets. *Pp.* 139-158.

CHAPTER XI.

ACROSS THE ALLEGHANIES.—Private Car—Harrisburg—Altoona—Underground Railway—Colt Shoe—Mountain House—Pittsburg—Natural Gas.
Pp. 159-176.

CHAPTER XII.

TO CHICAGO.—Indianapolis—Lake Michigan—The City—Church Conference—Fire-proof Buildings—The Great Fire—Dynamite Scare—Natural and Spiritual Light. *Pp.* 177-189.

CHAPTER XIII.

TO THE MISSISSIPPI.—Pacific Hotel—The Prairie—Schools—Milwaukee—Dawn on the Mississippi—Dangers—Minnesota—Minneapolis—Minnehaha—Falls of St. Anthony. *Pp.* 190-207.

CHAPTER XIV.

TO KANSAS CITY.—St. Paul—Plymouth Church—Navigation of Mississippi—Touch of Arctic Frost—State of Iowa—Missouri—Growth of Kansas City—Its Coloured People. *Pp.* 208-224.

CHAPTER XV.

FROM THE WEST.—St. Louis—Meeting of the Waters—Springfield of the West—Our own Line—Hammond Village—Testing Ride—Pittsburg Again—Portrait of Dr. Taylor. *Pp.* 225-240.

CHAPTER XVI.

WASHINGTON.—The Susquehanna—First View of the City—The Monument—The White House—The President—The War Reproduced—The Capitol—Culture of the Coloured People. *Pp.* 241-255.

CHAPTER XVII.

HOMEWARD.—Baltimore—Jersey Ferry by Night—Prayer Meeting—Banquet at Union League Club—The Parting—Gloomy Skies—The Gale—The Calm—The Welcome Home. *Pp.* 256-272.

CHAPTER I.

The Voyage.

T was blowing great guns when we reached Liverpool, on Wednesday the 8th September, 1886, to sail on the following afternoon for New York, by the s.s. *Republic*. All the way from the North the valleys had echoed the roar of the blast, and the tall trees bent before it like willow wands. The rain fell in torrents, and streams, usually unnoticed, dashed by our side as foaming cataracts. Everything wore a wintry aspect when we found shelter for the night under the hospitable roof of a relative of our friend Dr. Taylor, of Broadway Tabernacle, who was to be our fellow-voyager and our host in the New World. At the landing-stage, and on board the tender which was to take us to our ship, we had many cordial greetings from members of the doctor's former congregation in Liverpool, most of whom we had met in the days of his pastorate there. We were also delighted to find one or two connected

with our own neighbourhood, who happened to be in the city and sought us out. It was a pleasant parting, furnishing the opportunity of renewing old friendships, and was accompanied with introductions to officers and passengers, with whom new ties were to be formed. The gloomy skies were forgotten, and we were full of hope and joy.

The beginning of the voyage was not smooth. We were rocked all night, but not to infants' slumbers. Few were found on the deck, when, with the morning, we looked on the shores of old Ireland. What had been going on in the several state-rooms we partially heard, and may be imagined. There was a short respite, however, in the quiet waters of Queenstown Bay—a name familiar to those connected with the sea as the place where vessels call for orders on returning home; and as the only port touched in going on or returning from such a voyage as ours. Nearly all on board revived, charmed with the scenery, and welcoming the tender as it came alongside with news, not only the latest, but the last we would receive for fully a week.

We had here a proof of Irish enterprise, and the desire to push an honest trade, in the vendors of lace, staffs, deck-chairs, fruits, etc., who literally pushed their wares from the paddle-box of the tender to our deck. One earnest old woman, who could not find a place on the paddle-box, showed her ingenuity by having a line fixed to our bulwarks, and thereby hoisting her basket on board for our inspection. As it was understood that we would be delayed here for three or four hours, a few of the passengers went on shore, and took a run to Cork by rail. Whether they embraced the opportunity also of kissing the Blarney Stone we did not learn; but they had ample time to do so, and some thought there were signs afterwards that this had not been neglected.

We received the mails at Queenstown, the bags on this occasion being specially numerous—about 600 —as the previous steamer, which should have taken a portion of them, had been disabled. These we watched with interest as one by one they were counted, and tossed, by no means tenderly, into our hold. They were addressed to all parts of America, from New York to California; and also to Australia and New Zealand. Some time ago, at Dover, we noticed the mails for the Antipodes put on board to go Eastward, and here were those intended to reach the same destination by going Westward. How extremes meet! How small, too, the world must be when we can salute our kindred at the extremities of the empire by stretching our hands both to the right and to the left, as if embracing the whole sphere in our arms! And, surely, if one arm goes out from Dover, it is only proper that the other should go out from Queenstown. This, besides keeping Ireland near our heart, has obvious practical advantages which she may justly claim as due to her position, being nearer America than any other part of the British Isles. The changes lately made by our Post Office authorities, depriving Ireland in part of a privilege she has so long enjoyed, though to some extent afterwards recalled, are not unnaturally a new source of grievance which it would have been well to have avoided, and which it would be well not to carry further than the public interests absolutely demand.

The beauty of Queenstown Bay, surrounded by bold head-lands, and green hills dotted with white cabins, or clothed with wood, while the town itself rises in terraces on the more distant heights, made one quite fall in love with the Emerald Isle. And this impression was not effaced as we left the bay, and sailed along the south-western shore, discovering little villages nestling among the hills, with the iron-bound coast broken into beautiful, or wild and fantastic forms, by the relentless ocean. Our attention here was arrested by a little rocky island, from which an old castle seemed to rise in calm defiance. An artist might well sketch it as a picturesque example of the round-tower period. We were told, however, that both castle and rock are one—a natural formation, and an impregnable barrier against the billows. Would that our Irish friends were thus connected with the Eternal Rock! How safe would be their position, and how easily might their wrongs be then set right!

We lingered on the deck, after the darkness had set in, and watched, with mingled feelings, the last light-house, as it disappeared in the distance, or dipped beneath the horizon. Softly, my little fellow-voyager and I, in a quiet corner, hymned the words, "Star of peace gleam on the billow," and other songs of the sea, with a depth of meaning they never had before, and with calm sweet trust. How cheering it was to believe that we had not set out on a dark and shoreless ocean, but that the new world, though as yet unknown to us, was as certainly on the other side, as the old and familiar was on this! So may it be when we leave that shore to which no voyager returns!

And now we were on the bosom of the broad Atlantic; not so gentle as we could have wished, and whose heaving brought many a sigh. There was a sad display of empty seats at breakfast, and a yet sadder at dinner. The "souls" of many "abhorred all manner of meat;" and I confess that, on a certain occasion, I was one of them. Sabbath, our third day at sea, was the beginning of comparative peace. Dr. Taylor preached to a fair representation of passengers who could venture to the saloon, while I undertook a similar duty in the steerage. Neither was conducted without difficulty, as one had to steady both body and mind at the same time. But there was a reward in the interest taken in the services, and, we trust, in something better.

Gradually, day by day, the skies brightened, and the sea settled, till "the blue above and the blue below" seemed to vie with each other to obtain our admiration. We entered the Gulf Stream, and the temperature rose rapidly. The deck became a scene of life and joy, seldom interrupted afterwards by any change of weather. Ladies and gentlemen lounged in their deck-chairs, basking in the sun, or, under the shadow of an awning, reading, writing, chatting, or gazing silently, in vacant abstraction, on the glittering sea. Some, with evident relish, were sipping their chicken soup or beaf-tea, handed round the saloon-deck between breakfast and luncheon, to mitigate the craving which the other four meals seemed unable to satisfy. A child careered along with skipping ropes; others, of larger growth, seeking to renew their youth by also trying their feet. The young men attempted cricket, ingeniously providing against the lack of space by fixing their ball with a string to a spar. Both elder and younger took to a kind of curling, using *wooden* stones; or to a kind of quoits, using rings of *rope*, which they sought to put on a wooden pin. Familiarity grew, and the young ladies were sometimes induced to join the young gentlemen in these games, or to walk with them in a brotherly and sisterly spirit!

The sights without were few, but yet sufficient to break the monotony of the boundless expanse. There might be seen, occasionally, a lonely Mother-Cary's chicken flitting swallow-like over the wave; a few porpoises chasing us, and, in their zeal, springing entirely out of the water; a shoal of whales, causing spray like the splash of a cannon ball, some lifting their huge backs, and displaying their tails, within gun-shot, to the great delight of the passengers; or, general interest was excited by one or two homeward-bound vessels coming so close as not only to receive a salute by the dipping of our ensigns but by the waving of our handkerchiefs. It was a fine sight to meet a sailing ship, with every inch of canvass stretched, moving slowly, but majestically, with more dignity, if less defiant of the elements, than the *Servia*, which, in full steam, had just crossed us.

There were also various sounds, which broke the "silence of the sea." There were the half-hour watch-bells, the larger responding to the smaller, telling each other and us of passing time; the boatswain's whistle, calling his men around him to some special work; the sailors' song, enabling them to give a strong pull, a long pull, and a pull altogether; the "All's well," echoing through the stillness of the night, and soothing us to peaceful slumber; and the gong, rousing the sleepers, or inviting the hungry to welcome supplies.

But there was another sound, widely contrasted with these, that of the horrid steam fog-horn, startling us with its sudden yell and deep hollow groan. This was particularly *eerie* at night, suggesting the possibility of no very pleasant encounters; and too frequent, for our comfort, off the banks of Newfoundland. An anxious passenger, who imagined that the expression 'off the banks' implied a nearness to some shore, asked the captain, to whom he had previously been somewhat troublesome, if we were far from land. "Less than a mile," was the curt reply. Astonishment and alarm were immediately manifest. "Yes," responded the captain, "but it's down there," pointing to the bottom of the sea. "Off the banks" we were, in reality, about two hundred miles from land, though the depth might not be more than seventy or eighty fathoms. It was interesting, when the fog disappeared and the sun shone out, to see several fishing boats carrying on their craft, and, with furled sails, rolling on the smooth swell of the ocean. We noticed two small rowing boats, far from their parent vessels, looking like lost wanderers, forgetful of poor Richard's words :—

> " Vessels large may venture more,
> But little boats should keep near shore."

After sunset we often paced the deck, admiring the ever-varied waving sheen which was cast by the moon on the silver sea. The evenings, however, were generally spent in the saloon, where at times all consciousness of motion seemed to cease, with the exception of the slight tremor produced by the screw; so that we could scarcely imagine we were not in a spacious and well-provisioned hotel on shore. Here we found every possible comfort, and numerous sources of instruction and recreation. Draught-boards were often in use, earnest and lively conversations engaged in, books read, little groups propounding and solving puzzles, or the piano was played, with sometimes a sweet voice, or blended voices, warbling over all. We had also a concert, advertised by little volunteers appearing as sandwich men, announcing that the performance would be by "black albinoes, admission free, children half price."

It was thus that our gallant ship, with the days and nights glided swiftly on, till we began to look out for the land. We were apprised of our position daily at noon, when latitude and longitude, with distance run, were laid down on a little chart fixed on the companion-way. The chart was an object of great interest, and its coming contents a subject of earnest speculation, followed by congratulations or condolence as the speed exceeded or came short of our calculations.

A sad sight was witnessed after our position was marked for the last time, and while we were yet a long way from land. The top masts of a vessel, with the spars still clinging to them, were seen rising twenty or thirty feet out of the water. These belonged to the ill-fated *Oregon*, one of the most magnificent of the Cunard Liners, which lay, as yet unbroken, in the depths beneath. She sunk here, on the night of the 14th March, 1886, when those on board were suddenly aroused from their slumbers by her striking into a vessel, declared to have been unseen at the moment, and never discovered afterwards. There had been barely time to take to the boats, in which hundreds floated helplessly, and apparently hopelessly, in the gloom. Fortunately the sea was calm, and, with the morning, all were picked up by a passing vessel. We sailed so near the wreck that we could distinguish the ropes hanging uselessly which had so lately bound the rigging firmly together. The spot was guarded by a lightship, but withal it was not very safe. As we looked at these sad top-masts, like the fingers of one drowned which alone had reached the surface, lifted up in vain for help, a silent thoughtfulness crept over the passengers, thus reminded of the perils of the deep; and, we trust, feeling grateful to Him who had so marvellously provided deliverance on that terrible night, and had, not less wonderfully, preserved us hitherto from all accident.

Shortly after passing the wreck of the *Oregon*, we were cheered by several visitors from land—butterflies of various hues, driven or enticed, from their fragrant moorings, far to sea, and clinging to our bare boards for refuge. Some were easily caught, and we could not refrain from securing one or two as curiosities in the circumstances; but others, the brightest and strongest of wing, escaped, doubtless to perish more miserably on the wave.

Our last sun at sea was now sinking in the horizon. It was directly a-head, and some of us hastened to the prow, which seemed as if it were about to cut into the glowing orb. We gazed, shading our eyes, like Columbus,

"Who push'd *his* prows into the setting sun,"

in the hope of seeing the New World beyond. It was

dark, however, before we were gratified; and, like the great discoverer, it was by the lights on the shore we knew that land was there. These lights consisted of the brilliant lamps, electric and otherwise, from the spacious hotels and terraces of Coney Island—the great watering-place of New York—which gradually opened up to us like a string of pearls. They seemed long to linger in view, with apparently little change of position, as we rounded *Sandy* Hook—the *Scotchman* whom an American brother says he always sees first on returning home, and last on leaving it.

At length we drop anchor in the bay, at the mouth of the broad and beautiful harbour of New York. This bay furnishes at once a direct connection with, and a partial protection from the Ocean. The City, though only a few miles distant, is yet unseen. One or two local steamers are anchored near us, whose windows, all aglow with variously-coloured lights, seem, in the still waters, "to float double, ship and shadow." A small boat had approached, and hails us out of the darkness, when we distinguish the voices, though not the forms, of sons of mine host. They had taken a long journey through the city, and a long pull through the sea, that, with the earliest opportunity, they might cheer us with good news from their home, and learn if all was well with us on board. Their merry voices break for a little the stillness, but gradually die in the distance, as they hasten to relieve and gladden anxious friends. Custom House and Quarantine regulations forbid that we should land with them. Looking forward, however, with perfect confidence to the welcome immediately before us, we patiently wait for the breaking of the day.

And thus ended our voyage, on the 18th of Sept., eight days after the last land was left, and nine after we had left Liverpool. It had not been without a little roughness in the beginning, but how blessed throughout, and how peaceful in its close! May it be so with the great voyage of life! And may we find, on "death's dark night," bright lights and familiar voices from the Better World, turning its gloom into gladness, and see the day about to dawn when we shall enter "through the gates into the City!"

CHAPTER II.

New York and its Churches.

WITH the dawn of the Sabbath, the land we had so earnestly looked for opened upon us. Fit day for the first time to gaze on a New World, and tread its shores! A slight mist, from the early heat, hung on the calm waters, and partially veiled the prospect. But this only added to the charm, giving scope for the imagination to magnify the beauties of the scene, and picture it with fairer forms than its own. All things seemed to enjoy the day of rest; and even our good ship steamed gently and noiselessly along, as if it, too, had respect for the hallowed morn, and was reluctant to break the stillness.

Passing through the Narrows—the gates of the city, powerfully guarded by Fort Richmond and Fort Hamilton—the broad harbour of New York was discovered. It seemed somewhat to resemble that of Queenstown in form, but evidently excelled it in space, and presented a striking contrast in signs of an overflowing population and commercial industry. Directly in front of us was the city itself, rising on a tongue of land where the Hudson and East Rivers meet. The Produce Exchange, the Washington Buildings, and the graceful spire of Trinity Church, stood out most prominently as nearest us and in themselves most lofty, while a vast wilderness of houses crowded thickly behind. To the right was Brooklyn, attracting our attention chiefly by the famous Bridge which joins it to New York, spanning the East River (at that point nearly half-a-mile broad), but also extending into a portion of both cities, so that the entire length of the bridge is fully a mile and a-half. Its lofty towers, toward their bases, were lost in the mist, but, as they rose above the river, they were clearly relieved on the sky; while the great iron cables supporting the ways, and the ways themselves, seemed, from our distance, as gossamer threads, and the whole as if suspended in mid-air. To the left was Jersey City, with the heights behind, separated from New York by the Hudson; here at its mouth about a mile broad, and merged in the great harbour, or rather chiefly instrumental in making it.

Towering up toward the Jersey side, about half a mile from it, and fully a mile and a-half from the New York and Brooklyn sides, is the famous Statue of Liberty; the gift of the French, but chiefly paid for by the Americans. It stands on a massive pedestal built on a little island called Bedloe's, and is certainly the most prominent object in the whole harbour, conspicuous not only on entering, but from all directions. It is a colossal female figure, holding in one hand a tablet with the date 4th July, 1776, affixed to it—the day of the Declaration of Independence—and in the other a torch raised aloft with strained arm. The torch is 350 feet above the sea; higher than our loftiest spires, and about as high as is the golden cross of St. Paul's above the marble pavement. When we saw the figure first, the head had yet to be put on (neither Monarchy nor Republic can do without that), and its place was indicated by bars of iron or brass, through which the light of day appeared. Now that it is complete, as we afterwards saw it, the best brains of the country may enter, and a score of senators hold a council within its brazen skull; or they may look through those wondrous eyes on the commerce coming from all nations, and see their own wealthiest and most populous cities lying at their feet.

The Statue of Liberty may not add anything to the pleasing effect produced on entering this picturesque bay, but it at least furnishes a most striking feature. And, although most gigantic, it is not out of proportion to a harbour which embraces a body of water about two miles in diameter, with two broad rivers stretching far inland, to the north and east, along which innumerable wharves and docks are ranged. I may here remark, that the part of the Hudson included in the harbour furnishes thirteen miles of wharfage, that of the Harlem river fully two miles; and the East river furnishes upwards of nine miles; each wharf capable of receiving vessels of the greatest tonnage. The entire harbour, within the Narrows, contains fully a hundred and fifteen square miles of water, completely land-locked, yet in safe and immediate communication with the ocean at all seasons, and where nearly all the fleets of the world might find a convenient anchorage.

As we approach the wharf of the White Star Line, of which our good ship the *Republic* is one, we distinguish on it the family whose home we sought, waving us the welcome, which soon we receive in a warm grasp, and afterwards under their hospitable roof. Before leaving the wharf, however, our honesty, and submission to tariff law, had to be tested by a searching examination at the Custom House. This was a much more severe and trying ordeal than I had anticipated. Everything we possessed had to be turned up and turned out. But nothing objectionable was found among us, and we were allowed to pass, after much time and patience had been exhausted. How well to be able, and know that we are able, to stand such a test as that, and another vastly more momentous that is yet before us all!

We were in excellent time for the morning services in Broadway Tabernacle, and engaged in them with as much comfort as if we had come from a refreshing sleep in our own home; and we trust with special profit,

"Praising the Lord for His goodness." Dr Taylor did not preach on this occasion, as it was uncertain when he might return, and other arrangements had been made. We sat, therefore, together in the pew on this my first Sabbath in America, as we sat together in the pulpit on my last.

Broadway Tabernacle is a very handsome structure, with massive tower and lofty pointed roof. Its main front is toward the street which gives it its name, just at the point where it intersects the Sixth Avenue at an acute angle; making a fine open space, the breadth of the two streets. It extends also a good way into 34th Street, where are commodious halls for Sabbath Schools, prayer meetings, etc. The advantages of its situation, however, and its external beauty, are somewhat marred by the nearness of the elevated railway. The interior has a remarkably pleasing, as well as an imposing effect, with spacious area and galleries and lofty ceiling. The organ rises from behind the pulpit to the top of the ceiling in three tiers, tastefully ornamented and coloured. There is a select choir of eight, four of the voices occasionally singing an anthem, to which the congregation most attentively listen. In this manner the services are always opened, and the music is of the very best, in selection and performance. But I must confess I would rather the first place was given to the grand outburst which was heard afterwards, when the vast congregation sung most heartily, guided and sustained by the organ and complete choir. I need not say that the preacher is at home in his own pulpit, where his power and popularity are not less than when he draws together, and deeply impresses, crowded congregations in the old country. His people were gradually returning to the city after their holidays, and by the end of October they were well out, while numerous strangers waited in the sheltered porch till seat-holders were accommodated. The sittings are about 1700, but I believe in a pressure the church could hold about 2000.* Gas and electric lights are both used, the latter particularly welcome for its coolness, as well as for its superior brilliancy. The heat was great, even in October, and sometimes in September it had been 90°. Hence fans were in constant use, and it seemed as if a flock of doves was ever fluttering all around us. The pulpit was supplied with the same cooling instrument, only larger than the others, in proportion to the honour and prominence of the position.

I had the privilege of participating in the Sacrament of the Lord's Supper with the congregation over which Dr. John Hall presides. The building is

---

* The congregation of Broadway Tabernacle has an annual income of about 36,000 dollars, raised entirely from pew rents, for the support of ordinances; and upwards of 33,000 dollars for missionary and benevolent purposes, raised by collections and subscriptions. The total last year was 69,263 dollars, that is about £14,000. At the morning service on the 24th March, 1887, in connection with the fifteenth anniversary of Dr. Taylor's pastorate in New York, in half-an-hour the sum of 35,000 dollars was subscribed, or put in the plate in cash, by which the entire debt remaining on the building was swept away; and at his tenth anniversary, five years ago, between 30,000 and 35,000 dollars were raised, and handed over for the building of the Bethany Church and Schools, which are supported by the congregation.

one of the ornaments of the city, said to be the largest, and perhaps the handsomest, Presbyterian Church in the world. So far as my experience goes, I am inclined to subscribe to this statement, though some may think it only yielding to an Americanism. It is situated in the Fifth Avenue—the finest street in New York—where its spire rises gracefully above the splendid private buildings, palatial hotels, and the other magnificent churches which adorn that neighbourhood. The interior is lined almost entirely with wood, unpolluted by paint; the organ, pulpit, galleries, and pews being of the same material, which has a warm, pleasing tone, not unlike sandal-wood, and chastely carved. There is no choir, and it is rather odd to see the precentor perched aloft above the minister, yet raising his lonely voice, clear and loud, over all the mechanical harmony behind him, and courageously leading the thousand voices before him and beneath. I had the honour previously of being introduced to Dr. Hall, and, in turn, at the close of the services, was introduced to his elders, some of whom he was pleased to say were from Scotland, and they were equally pleased to acknowledge their nationality. He mentioned that he had been mistaken more than once for our greatest Scottish preacher, Dr. Cairns, and felt the honour. His manner, however, in the pulpit differs considerably from our Principal's, being comparatively quiet, and not without a flavour from the Emerald Isle, where he was so long popular; but his frame has some resemblance, as he is tall, well proportioned, and manly. He is also a most effective preacher.

It was very gratifying to see how these two congregations—Broadway Tabernacle and Fifth Avenue Presbyterian—the largest and most influential in the city, excepting it may be in some respects Trinity Church, were drawn together, and kept together, by the preaching of the pure old gospel, of which Paul was not ashamed. The work which they accomplish in and beyond their own borders in New York, also in extending the gospel to the West, as well as among the heathen in other lands, is invaluable. Many congregations in the city are at one with them in spirit, and nearly abreast with them in Christian usefulness.

I had the privilege of meeting several of their ministers of different denominations. Through Dr. Taylor I was introduced to about twenty of these at the weekly gathering of a clerical Society known as the *Chi Alpha*. It met, on this occasion, in the house of the Rev. Dr. Prentiss, whose wife, now deceased, was the authoress of the well-known work, "Stepping Heavenward." He himself is a gentleman of marked ability and brotherly spirit. After a feast to the body, and a feast of cordial fellowship, there was an able paper read by Dr. Chambers on the "Relation of the Parables," and free conversation regarding it. Among the brethren present was Dr. Schaff, so widely known in this country, as well as in

America, for his original writings and scholarly
editions of German works. He is now showing
in his locks the snows of many winters, but his
countenance beams with genial kindness, and he
takes a warm interest in all the great questions of the
day on both sides of the Atlantic. I also met
occasionally with such men as Dr. Ormiston,—who took
part in the General Presbyterian Council in Edinburgh,
an able preacher and writer, most enthusiastic, generous,
warm-hearted, and truly brotherly; and Dr. Parkhurst
(who was with us on the *Republic*), an accomplished
scholar, with an important charge in New York.

These are all faithful ministers, and men of culture—Broad Church only in the sense of having an
extensive acquaintance with modern as well as with
ancient literature, and in co-operating with other denominations in all kinds of Christian work; not shallow,
however, as are many who claim to be broad, but deep
and clear in their religious convictions. And they are
but a specimen, though a very fair one, of a numerous
and noble band of zealous labourers who are building
up the Church of Christ, and are seeking to stem the
flood of religious error and of irreligion which is constantly flowing into the vast and rapidly increasing
population of this great city, now considerably over a
million and a-half. They are also imparting to multitudes who land, and have often to linger here on their
way to the Far West, spiritual blessings which may be
borne with them to the regions beyond. Such ministers

occupy what is, in many respects, the most important and influential sphere of Christian usefulness in the world, situated as it is at the entrance to this great continent, and virtually its capital. It is cheering and hopeful to contemplate their character and spirit, and the success which has already crowned their labours.

I looked into a congregation of coloured people, whose open door, and sweet music, drew me in toward the close of their services. The Sabbath School children were there, in the midst of their parents and friends, and apparently leading the praise. The music was lively, but by no means boisterous, and truly sacred, though lacking in harmony. I understood, by an intimation from the pulpit, that it was the custom to have the children thus brought together once a month. I saw no pale faces among them, though there was every shade of black. But, by the way, they are never in any case called black, or negro, but coloured people: anything else would be an offence, as it would not have been in the days of slavery, an offence which is seldom if ever given, except in wrath. They are free, also, to mingle with the white people in church, which, to a limited extent they do, sometimes as members; and I have often seen them in cars, where they were always treated with respect. Still they prefer to draw together and worship with their own people; just as it was with the Jews of various nationalities who came to reside at Jerusalem, which had each its separate synagogue; and as it is with Scotch Highlanders who have congregations of their own in our principal towns. No doubt the difference of language has something to do with these other separations, but not more perhaps than with that of the coloured people, who understand their ministers as they cannot understand the English of the learned.

I need not attempt to give anything like a general survey of the ecclesiastical condition of New York. This would be a ponderous task, as there are nearly five hundred churches in the city, representing most of the denominations known among ourselves, and others of which we happily know nothing. But I may remark here that the supply of religious ordinances throughout the States is very extensive. However it may be in the remoter West, when proceeding to the centre of the Continent I did not see a single village, even though it might not consist of more than a score of houses, in which a church was not to be found. A pioneer pastor often volunteers to leave a flourishing congregation, which he may have established in the East, and the larger congregations assist in building a church for him in the West, where, at the time, no village even existed, but where soon farmers and others congregate and erect dwellings; so that the supply is sometimes created before the demand. It is humorously said that to raise a church or a circus in the midst of a scattered settlement is the sure means of raising a township. No doubt there are some instances in which too many new causes are formed, and others in which the prevalence of infidelity, chiefly German, proves, for a while, a great hindrance. But these are exceptional cases, and one of them, at least, is not without its hopeful aspect in a growing country.

As a whole, the progress of Christian enterprise, and the planting and maintaining of new churches, is a special feature of American life. The members in full communion in all the Protestant Churches have increased last year by fully half a million. The Presbyterians alone, who are not the most numerous of the Protestant denominations, have more than 12,000 congregations, and raised, during last year, 780,000 dollars for foreign missions. Is not this something to fill every friend of religious truth and progress with hope, especially in the circumstances? When we remember the difficulties to be encountered, arising from the vast extent of the country, the scattered character of so much of its population, and the fact that every cause has to be begun at its foundation, chiefly by persons gathered together who were previously total strangers to each other: and when we know how many go there from other lands seeking for worldly wealth alone, or with a bitter hatred of all religion, which they identify with tyranny and superstition, or seeking refuge from the consequence of past crimes, and carrying much of the spirit of these with them, we cannot but look on the success of Christianity in America as furnishing a noble illustration of the power of Divine truth, and of the blessed fruits produced by a Free Church in a Free State. We only require to be on the spot and see these things, in order to be amazed, if not amused, at the fears of some good people that the Christian Church could not support itself, or would suffer, instead of being greatly blessed, by doing so. It is when the towing line is thrown off, and the noble ship, with outspread sails and engines at work, depends entirely on the breezes from heaven, and the heat from the glowing furnaces within, that she goes forth with power and grandeur, making progress which would be looked for in vain so long as she clung to tug or tender for aid. The anxieties on this point remind me of those of a lady, who had ventured to sea in a small boat, when a little breeze sprung up, and she said tremulously to the boatman, "Is there no fear?" "Yes," he replied, "there is plenty of *fear*, but no *danger*."

CHAPTER III.

New York Schools.

E visited one of the Public Schools in New York. There were 700 girls on the first floor, and 680 boys on the second. Other schools in the neighbourhood are much larger, one having about 1800 boys; but we may safely take this as a typical case—examples, conducted on similar principles, and in a similar manner, being common throughout the city, and also in cities and country towns, and even in comparatively lonely prairies, all over the States.

When we entered the boys' department the opening services had just been concluded, the Bible had been read, and the large volume was lying open on the desk of the head-master. It was charming not only to see how rapidly and orderly the children were divided into classes, but how the school-room itself was, at the same time, split into numerous portions. Double doors of frosted glass, and curtains suspended on brass rods, were drawn together, and fourteen separate apartments formed in a few seconds, as if by the rod of the enchanter, where as many classes met, entirely isolated from each other in sight, and almost entirely isolated in sound. We heard most of these examined, and put a few questions to them ourselves, finding the scholars well up in English, and in other important branches. I was particularly struck with their knowledge of the constitution of their own country; an attainment not so common as it should be among our children, either in regard to the American Republic or the British Monarchy. I may notice that it was not on a special occasion that we visited the school, but quite unexpectedly, and not to hear lessons specially prepared, but in the ordinary course. We learned, however, that it was no exceptional favour that was granted us in being present, but a privilege extended to all, who are at liberty to look into these schools at any time.

The ages of the boys seemed to range from eight years to eighteen; and yet, strange enough, of the fourteen teachers engaged only four were males, in addition to other two gentlemen who came, at certain hours, to teach German and drawing. It is not wonderful that in mixed classes the female teachers should predominate, as is often the case among ourselves, but that it should be so in schools composed entirely of boys, and these not always of tender years, is the peculiarity in this case. I can well believe that the ladies will have as much influence and authority over the boys as the gentlemen will have, perhaps even more, besides exercising greater patience with the younger ones. I heard a boy, who had been thus trained, say, "that he always felt so bad when he behaved ill to a lady, and that the other boys would taunt any one who showed disrespect towards her." May it be on this account that there is no corporal punishment in these schools? At all events there is none, other means of correction being taken; and when a boy becomes refractory, or refuses to attend, he is expelled; and if he refuses to go elsewhere, or repeats the same misconduct in another school, he is sent to a Reformatory. I was informed by a member of the New York Educational Department that he had a proposal before that body to establish a Reformatory for truants alone, so as to prevent them coming in contact with the criminal classes, and where they might be more freely, as well as more safely sent.

The education is compulsory, but the consequences of failure thus fall on the children, and not directly on the parents: the very fear of which must be a powerful corrective. We enquired of the headmaster of the school we visited regarding the attendance, and he put questions on this point to the various teachers in our presence. The result was that, out of classes of fifty or sixty, there were seldom more than two intimated as absent; and from these, in most cases, excuses had been sent which were felt to be quite satisfactory. And yet the morning was one continuous downpour of rain, such as I do not think I ever saw before ; what are usually separate drops coming down in apparently unbroken lines.

The education is also free in all branches, and in Normal Schools. The books are supplied by the Department, and only when wasted, or lost, are they required to be paid for by the pupils.

There is a species of drill in this, and the American Schools generally, to which, in Britain, we are not accustomed. A fire extincteur is to be found on every floor, and the young people are trained to its use, and also to the manner in which they may most safely escape from the premises in the event of fire. Experimental alarms are occasionally given ; it may be startling to strangers, but the evil of crying "wolf, wolf, when there is no wolf," is not felt by the children, as all are aware that the duty is the same, whether the alarm is real or imaginary. We are not so liable to danger from this cause as the Americans, but we have had sufficiently appalling accidents in factories and special gatherings of children, to render such a training by no means superfluous at home. It might make our enormous buildings for Public Schools all the safer, and form a habit of order and self-control in youth which might be of great service in later life.

The value of the system of public instruction throughout the United States, and its beneficial results on the nation at large, were borne witness to on all hands. Its grand aim is to fit the rising race to take their part as citizens in a country where, perhaps more than in any other, ignorance would be ruin. It seeks also to meet the case of the illiterate of riper years, such as those left among them as the fruits of slavery, or those totally uneducated coming among them from other lands, for whom evening classes are provided. In attaining these ends it is, at the same time, a powerful agent in welding together the various nationalities and classes of society, and in promoting among a people, where a great diversity of tongues prevails, the universal diffusion of the English language, the want of which is a serious defect in the Canadian system. The great difficulty experienced in this united effort, as in our own country, is in relation to the Roman Catholics, who are prevented, as far as possible, by their priests from attending these Public Schools. Still, many who desire a superior education for their children send them, so long as the denunciations from the altar are silent, or in proportion as the influence of the Hierarchy is melting away.

The religious education in all national schools, both at home and abroad, from the various denominations embraced, and the necessity of conserving all their interests, must be, to a large extent, nominal,

It is not possible, even if it were desirable, that it should be otherwise. To this the Christian people of America are fully alive, and hence the zeal they show in regard to Sabbath Schools, and the success which has attended their efforts. The best men in the country, prominent members of the Senate, and several of their presidents are, or have been, teachers. We were much pleased with the excellent halls, often most beautiful, as well as most commodious, provided for the children connected with each congregation, and generally built behind their churches. In these we found appliances not common with us, such as the very general use of the blackboard, on one of which we saw a drawing in coloured chalk which would have done credit to a first-class artist.

Flourishing Mission Schools also are provided for those whose parents may be connected with no particular congregation. We visited one of these, built and supported by the congregation of Broadway Tabernacle, and attended by about a thousand children, a large portion of whom were from the families of German artizans. The building is very convenient, as well as handsome, with every facility for carrying on the work, and is used also as a Mission Church. I found a novelty at the Mission School in the institution of a probation class, where new comers are kept for some two or three months before being admitted to all its privileges, such as books, soirees, and trips. An excellent American notion this, which,

if acted on universally at home, would correct many
abuses of those treats, and give the children to realize
that they were receiving a favour, and not giving one,
in coming for instruction. Another novelty I found
in a school where there was only one scholar allowed
in each class, and that a male, evidently not a junior,
with a female teacher to attend to him. These
couples may be seen dotted over the Hall every
Sabbath morning, and engaged in quiet converse
for about an hour before the church services. It is
a Chinese Sabbath School for men only, because
Chinese women are almost, if not entirely, unknown
in America; and for these individually, because of
their imperfect knowledge of the English language.

There are, in New York, ragged schools, and
schools for bringing the more abandoned under religious influence, which I regret I had not an opportunity of visiting. But I looked at some of the
localities from whence these are supplied. It might be
thought that a new country would not have given
time for such festering sores to spread; but it must
be remembered that many went, or were sent over,
chiefly from Ireland and Italy, who landed as
paupers, with neither strength nor energy to push
their way. It is chiefly in the neighbourhood of the
wharves the old parts of the city—that these are to
be found. There I saw lanes, resembling the closes
of Edinburgh and Glasgow, where cotton garments of
all kinds, and in various stages of decay, hung from

side to side of lofty buildings, seeking a little of the air that might come from the narrow strip above. Yet I must confess that even there I did not see anything of the extreme poverty often witnessed at home. I believe that wickedness and ungodliness reign in New York, and other cities of the Union, most powerfully where poverty is unknown.

In Sabbath School literature America is specially rich. There are innumerable magazines, tracts, leaflets, maps, cards, &c., most of them very beautifully illustrated, and often in colours, for the children. There are also magazines, weekly, monthly, and quarterly, containing instructive illustrations, for the teachers. I took an opportunity of purchasing a supply to take home as specimens, and found that of teachers' magazines alone I had fully a score of all sizes, and published in different quarters, sometimes bearing the names of certain cities or towns, and sometimes the names of certain denominations, as indicating their origin. All of these contain notes on the International Lessons; one portion of the same magazine being occupied occasionally with explanations of a scholarly kind, and another with examples and anecdotes to illustrate the lesson, and each having the scripture passage for the day printed both in the old and new versions, and embodying roll books, blackboard examples, and various other hints and helps for teachers. I found a column in the roll books in which attendance at church was to be marked, a hint that might be useful elsewhere. In every way one is impressed with the energy, enterprise, and liberality manifested throughout the States in seeking to train the rising generation in the knowledge of divine truth, and to bring them under its power.

There is another department of religious instruction which I must notice—the Young Men's Christian Association. I visited the building, at the corner of Fourth Avenue and 23rd Street. It is a very spacious and imposing edifice, containing five flats, and we ascended the various stages by means of an elevator. It is said not to be smaller than the Post Office. There is a Hall capable of accommodating fifteen hundred; and in all directions are rooms for various meetings, classes, lectures, reading, devotion, discussion, gymnastics, &c., all controlled by Christian men (who require to be members of some evangelical denomination,) and conducted on Christian principles. Their own division of their work, according to a programme for the winter, is social, literary, musical, educational, physical, and religious; opening up, it will be seen, a wide field. We observed a goodly number of young men, and old too, in the reading-room; and we were surprised at the extent of the library, with the value and costliness of many of its books. In works of general reference it seems exceptionally well furnished. We were shown several old versions of the Scriptures, and fac-similes of ancient manuscripts, volumes such as we only expect to find in the British Museum.

It is calculated that upwards of eight hundred persons enter the rooms of this institution every day, that over one hundred thousand come to the reading-room every year, and about thirty thousand to the library and gymnasium. These Young Men's Christian Associations, whilst they originated in Britain, have spread in America as they have done nowhere else; and upwards of a hundred buildings have been erected there for their use, with other Associations not so accommodated as yet, all linked together by some tie of federation.

CHAPTER IV.

New York—Work and Ways.

MONG the places of business in New York that specially interested me, were the printing and publishing premises of Harper Brothers, the most extensive and widely-known of the kind in the New World, if not also in the Old. They are situated in Franklin Square, and thus, at least nominally, connected with the father of typography in America. It is a hard forenoon's toil, forgotten in the pleasure, to go over these works; and we regret that we can do little more than allude to the visit we made to them in the company of one whose well-known face we had begun to find was an "Open Sesame" everywhere. We could fain pause to describe the army of compositors, the numerous presses of the newest construction pouring forth their contents like a waterfall, and yet allowing nothing to fall, but folding up every sheet speedily and with care; the machines for

wire-sewing, for cutting, for smoothing; the process of marbling paper, and of bookbinding in all its branches, from the simple paper wrapper and strong school-book cover to the more expensive and elaborate work in Russian or Morocco; for everything is carried on here in connection with book-making; and, so long as some of the partners continue in the firm, authors will be found there too.

I was particularly drawn to the artistic department, not surely because it was marked "private," whatever curiosity we may have in our nature, but because I had long admired the gems that so profusely illustrate the serial and other works of the Harpers, and knew that they were looked on with envy by engravers in the old country. The drawings in crayon and ink, from the hands of the artists, were finished with great care, and were very beautiful; as was the process of engraving them on small separate blocks, afterwards so ingeniously joined together to make one picture. But the transferring of these again to metal plates to be directly used in printing, so that any number of impressions might be taken without injuring them, was most marvellous. We cannot, perhaps we dare not, without violating confidence, describe the details of this process, but we may say that it was a most elaborate and minute one, in which, among other machines, an electric battery was employed, so powerful, that, when the conductor was touched by a rod, the brilliant blue sparks emitted were accompanied by reports like those of a pistol, and the current was such that for any one to receive from it a shock would be instant death. Few among the many who admire the engravings in the works of the Harpers, so widely known now in this country, can have any idea of the time, and labour, and care expended in producing them.

The day of our visit was one on which the illustrated serials were being printed. These are: *The Bazaar*, chiefly intended for ladies; *The Weekly*, containing general information, with an allusion to passing events; *The Young People*, an exhaustless treasure for the children; and *The Monthly Magazine*, so well known for the valuable instruction it imparts on all subjects, and the delightful tours it takes us over all lands. Of this last, we were told, upwards of 70,000 are circulated in this country, and upwards of 140,000 in America, every month. It was a great treat to my young companion from Scotland to see *her* magazine, so long a favourite, being printed; and a still greater treat for her to spend an afternoon in the home and with the family of the accomplished editor—one of the partners of the firm, who makes this work truly a labour of love. I was much gratified to be introduced to the Harper Brothers, men of superior intelligence, young, genial, and enthusiastic in their profession. We learned something of the history of the firm, and were pleased to be shown the first volume which issued from their press, dated near the beginning of the century; the name on the title page then being the same as is to be found still, not retained officially, but as that borne by the relatives themselves, on whom the mantle of the founder has fallen. It was a religious work, and so far typical of the myriads of sheets they have scattered, and are, in ever-increasing numbers, scattering among the English-speaking nations. No sheet with the Harpers' names imprinted on it but may be introduced with safety into any home, where it is sure to shed 'sweetness and light.' May they be useful in binding these nations together in a growing love for pure literature, and in its universal diffusion!

Many of the other business premises of New York, like those I have just described, are most extensive. In height, especially, they are out of all proportion to those with which we are familiar at home. Some are eight, ten, and eleven storeys high, but as they display every variety of architecture, they are by no means unsightly edifices. The most numerous and imposing, as evidently those carrying on the greatest trade, are situated in Broadway. I visited several of these in calling on friends from our neighbourhood, and was pleased with the taste manifest in their interior fittings. I was charmed with the offices of G. A. Clark & Brother, connected with the well-known thread firm in Paisley. Some of their apartments were like drawing-rooms, and their samples were arranged most artistically in pleasing devices, all trouble in ascending their various floors to inspect these being avoided by that great American institution—the elevator. One felt especially at home here, where faces, long familiar, gave the cordial Scottish recognition and welcome.

I looked into some of the public buildings—most of them situated in or near Broadway—such as the Stock Exchange, which seemed like a lunatic asylum let loose, and the Bank, Post Office, Custom House, &c., but as these differ little from those at home I need not describe them. Luncheon rooms are in great demand in a city where so many business men have their dwellings at a distance. I was kindly entertained at one, where, I learned, about a thousand persons sat down daily. The hotels are enormous buildings, and, with all our efforts to cope with the Americans in this matter, not as yet exceeded by anything at home. They have generally large and gorgeous porches for lounging in, and conversing with visitors; and what we find at our railway stations, in the form of bookstalls and barbers' shops, are often under the roof of these porches; and we have also seen added elsewhere the apothecaries' hall. I was called to a private room in one of the city hotels to visit a brother in the ministry, Rev. A. Graham, of Crossgates, who had gone to Australia for his health, and was returning through the States, greatly shattered by the journey. It was touching to see the devotion of an English gentleman, previously a stranger, who had been introduced to him in Australia, and had accompanied him as a companion, friend, and helper all the way. We regretted to learn that Mr. Graham reached home only to die, leaving a sorrowing widow and family.

In regard to the streets of New York, they have several peculiarities which strike one from the old country. They are nearly all mathematically arranged at right angles, long and straight, having prosaic numbers to distinguish them instead of fancy names—those running north and south called avenues, and those running east and west called streets. This arrangement, however, if formal, has at least one most important practical advantage, as it indicates both the distance and the direction from place to place—for every twenty-one blocks measure about a mile—and thus a stranger is enabled to find his way, comparatively easily, through the city. Broadway alone, of all the streets of any length, during a great part of its course, refuses to submit to rule and compass after this fashion, and goes winding along at its own sweet will. It often cuts the other streets at acute angles, leaving open spaces, which are wisely added to and taken advantage of to form squares or corners, which are sometimes furnished with leafy foliage, where cool retreats may be found, and where one may sit or stroll under the shade, and view, in quiet and ·safety, the flood of human activity, with vehicles of every conceivable kind, passing by. Whilst this great and well-known street did not disappoint me in the enormous pressure and variety of the business it displayed, nor in the magnificent public buildings and other premises which line it on either side for fully half-a-dozen miles, yet I was somewhat disappointed with its breadth, as its name had led me to anticipate something greater in that direction than I found. It does not exceed, in this respect, some streets in the old country, and is far behind many in the new. The name, however, was evidently given to it in the early history of the city, when it was the great highway to the north, and contrasted with the narrow streets still existing near the wharves in the south; and, like all old roads, it had no love for the straight. Its total length, from the Battery Park to the outskirts, is fully nine miles.

The formality of the streets is not monotonous, or displeasing to the eye, for the ground is occasionally undulating, and the buildings are imposing and manifest great variety of architecture. Nothing can exceed the beauty of Fifth Avenue, in spite of its stretch for six miles in a direct line, and being closely built on either side. It is lined with lofty and most beautiful churches, grand hotels, ornamented after the manner of palaces, and private dwellings with oriels and doorways gracefully and elaborately carved. At certain hours it is busy as Broadway itself; not, however, with the restless hurry of those who hasten to make rich, but with the more leisurely movements of those who seek to display what has already been made. The wealth and fashion of the city pass along its centre, riding slowly on horseback, or reclining in splendid equipages and vehicles of every kind, closely crowded together; while pedestrians stroll on the pavements, where the ladies, in gayest attire, with parasols of every hue, appear like a border of tropical flowers blazing in the sunshine, or shaded now and again by some lovely trees. In the afternoons two streams flow unceasingly in opposite directions, the one going to and the other returning from the Park. It is the Rottenrow of New York, if we can speak of a *King's highway* where kings have never been. It lacks, indeed, the noble park throughout, with the parallel ways which make the London royal drive so charming. But it has its origin in a park of no little beauty, and ultimately passes along another, for nearly three miles, which cannot be excelled anywhere. And it has residences that may be truly called royal, such as that of the late Mr. Stewart, (which cost three million dollars), occupied, when we were there, by his lonely widow.

It is well that the Elevated Railroads, four in number, do not pass along Fifth Avenue or Broadway —though they go in the same direction—as they are no improvement to the appearance of the city. They run above the streets close to the pavements on either side, with bars stretched across, joining the up and down lines, so as to strengthen them. When you look along, between the lines, you seem to see an extensive well-lighted tunnel, crowded with cars, carts, &c. These railways are not quite so light as I had expected, the beams which support them being strong and massive. But they are not altogether unsightly, and they furnish a most comfortable and pleasing means of travelling in the heat of summer, besides being indispensable to a city fully eight miles in length, which must have either an upper or an underground railway; the former certainly much more agreeable to passengers than the latter. They are evidently very popular, for, if we are to believe an advertisement I saw in one of the carriages—meant to encourage business men to use them for advertising—there are 300,000 persons travelling by them every day.

There is one remarkable feat which these railways achieve. They occasionally cross from one street to another; and it is wonderful, if not alarming, in doing so, to see what sudden turns they will make. I have heard of a man who tried to construct a gun that would shoot round a corner, but the American engineers have shown themselves more than equal to this by making their trains run round one sharp corner, and then immediately turn round another, so that you sometimes see the carriage next you suddenly move off at a right angle from you to the one side, and then as suddenly take the same bend to the other side, and yet all the while your link is not broken.

If the Elevated Railroads are not an ornament to the city, neither are the telegraph poles, with innumerable wires attached, ranged along several of the principal streets. The authorities have evidently been impressed with this, as I observed the pavements in some places being lifted, and a space, their entire breadth and about two feet deep, being cleared, where the whole apparatus might be buried out of sight. Should this experiment succeed, furnishing sufficient isolation for the wires, it will be a vast improvement, both in appearance and convenience, and may well be adopted in our cities on this side of the Atlantic, where the wires, stretched from the roofs of houses, are more dangerous, if they are not so unsightly.

At the southern extremity of the city, on the spot where it had its origin by the settlement of the Dutch in 1614, is Battery Park, comparatively humble, but having an interest, besides this historical one, all its own. It has close behind it, and on either hand, the scenes of greatest business activity, being at the point where Broadway begins and the great Elevated Railways converge. Yet there is a certain seclusion about it, as nearly all these scenes are hid, though their hum is heard, behind the fine trees clothed in their richest verdure. Here the Hudson and East rivers meet, and it commands one of the liveliest and finest harbour scenes on which the eye could rest. Brooklyn and Jersey cities are within a mile on either side, and before you is the noble expanse of water opening wide and stretching some five miles to the Narrows, thence out to the ocean. You can rest on a seat, under the shade of one of these fine old trees, and look out on the perpetual motion of steam boats of all sizes, shooting in every direction, and on innumerable vessels gently gliding along; with the stable, if not the frowning form of Fort Columbus on the green banks of Governor's Island, appearing as the Guardian of all. The figure of the Statue of Liberty rises conspicuous, though nearly two miles distant, where the tallest masts are seen like those of the Lilliputians, with a Gulliver in the midst of them. More than once I lingered here alone, and I could have done so much oftener and longer had time permitted.

We had a delightful drive through the Central Park, which is certainly, in magnitude and variety, the finest I have ever seen. It contains 843 acres, being thus larger than any other park in Europe. It has 43 acres of lakes, ten miles of carriage drives, thirty miles of footpaths, with numerous statues of American and foreign celebrities, arranged so as to give many pleasing surprises. Along with the artificial there is much of the natural in the Park, consisting of various windings among rocky crags, or under shady cliffs—the whole constructed with wonderful skill, out of what was formerly wild marshy land. There are several lofty mansions in the neighbourhood, eight or ten storeys high, overlooking the whole scene, and Let, we understand, after the Scotch fashion, in flats; but these are so spacious that only the wealthiest can secure one. The plan of joint-occupancy has enabled the proprietors to erect buildings, in size and style of architecture, most imposing in their character, and adding to the dignity of the neighbourhood nearly as much as Buckingham Palace does to St. James' Park. It is remarkable, however, that only a little way off, where ground has been broken for new buildings, and some nearly finished, the most wretched hovels are to be found, unsurpassed by any Indian wigwam or Irish cabin. They have been pitched, and are still occupied, by squatters, with apparently a free, but doubtless a very uncertain, tenure. If such would be the result of a "no rent policy," better to have something to pay, if it would only be a motive to improvements; and if such would be the result of no security, as no doubt it is, better that farms were granted as feus than with such leases.

Leaving the Park, we continued our journey onwards to the banks of the Hudson, where, on the heights overlooking that broad and noble river, charming drives and boulevards are being extended, and fine villas built. What most interested me here, however, was the grave of General Grant. It is an arch, built on the side of a knoll, where the coffin is exposed to view, protected by iron and glass, with evergreens and flowers growing behind and twining themselves around it. Meanwhile it is guarded by soldiers night and day; but it is intended to build a monument on rising ground close at hand, where the body will have a permanent resting-place. From that position the many thousands who are continually sailing up and down the Hudson, may look, from near and far, on a spot sacred to the memory of one whose name stood out so prominently during the war of the Confederacy, who gained the greatest victories, dictated the terms of surrender to the conquered army, secured by the sword what Abraham Lincoln had proclaimed by the pen—the liberation of over three millions of slaves—and who was spared, as President, to render the most valuable assistance in healing the wounds of his bleeding country.

CHAPTER V.

Short Excursions.

 TRIP to Coney Island is a favourite one with the inhabitants of the three neighbouring cities, and with many throughout the States. The distance is about ten miles from New York, and is an easy run by rail from Brooklyn, or partly by rail and partly by boat.

We arranged to spend a forenoon on the shore here as a treat to a few young friends, and took the route in going that gave the benefit of the sail. We enjoyed the busy scene in the bay, of which one can never weary, alive with floating crafts of every kind, more numerous and more curious than I have ever seen elsewhere. But we were rather amused than favourably impressed on reaching the Brighton of America. It presents, indeed, a grand unbroken prospect of ocean, where the multitudes who crowd the beach—said to be about 70,000 daily—may breathe

the pure ozone, and bathe in the blue waters; precious blessings to those pent in these cities, especially during the heat of summer. There they may stand on the point of an iron pier, and find themselves a thousand feet at sea; or ascend to the top of an iron elevator—which rises open, slender, and doubtful, like four enormous ladders supported by leaning against each other—and look down on the azure blue three hundred feet above its surface. There they may enter inside an elephant, vastly more capacious than the wooden horse of Troy, and constructed of the same material, where hundreds can wander through limbs, and body, and trunk, making purchases of toys and trinkets; and from its great round eyes, and other openings, look above the various buildings around, and over a wide expanse both of land and sea. There, too, they may find ample accommodation in the enormous hotels to the east, or abundant supplies for the day in the restaurants to the west. In spite of all this, however, there is a lack of stability and dignity about the place. There are few, if any, private residences, and the buildings are mostly of wood, which gives one the idea of their being temporary; and, unhappily, the west end is supplied with menageries, merry-go-rounds, and all the paraphernalia of an English fair of pleasure, as a prominent feature. We saw it, however, under unfavourable circumstances, as the busy season, which continues only during the heat of summer, was about over, and there was a deserted look about it, "like a feast from which the guests have departed."

We returned by rail to Brooklyn. It was a novelty to pass by the fields of Indian corn, and see their tall, thick stems, with their fern-shaped but brown and solid leaves; while the reapers were *plucking* the baton-like ears, each clustered, more than a hundredfold, with yellow grains. There was not much of beauty otherwise in the scene, and what there might be was in no small degree marred by unsightly advertisements. This we came to discover was a characteristic, not only of the city, but also of the country, wherever any important road or railway might pass. Outhouses and farm-gables, in otherwise lonely parts, are painted black that they may have advertisements in white, or white that they may have them in black. Even pailings, that can stand letters, are all littered over: and we have seen noble rocks, rising grandly from a beautiful but well-frequented river, thus degraded by the brush. But the deformity seemed to reach its climax on the route from Coney Island, where some of the advertisements are monstrously colossal; one having letters each about the size of a cottage, set pretty widely apart, and extending along the open space for nearly a mile. Passing along one of the busy streets of Brooklyn, in front of a car, I saw a man, in full military costume, parading on the roof of a building, with a gun on his shoulder. I asked the driver what the soldier was guarding. "Guarding, Sir! he is an advertisement!" "Of what?" "To attract attention to the shop below, and to the advertisement on the gable behind." I have heard it said, that if an American succeeds in discovering the North Pole he will be sure to leave posted on it a notice of some one's pickles or pills. But, perhaps, we should not be too severe on this practice, as it is needful in a new country into which strangers are constantly flowing. Still it would be well if our cousins, in this matter, would keep within reasonable bounds.

Free from all such distractions, we had a delightful drive through Brooklyn Park on reaching that city by rail. This Park is not so extensive as the Central one, in New York; but I think it is scarcely less beautiful, and I believe it is larger than any other similar place of recreation anywhere else. It has eight miles of drive, and eleven of walks, embracing 550 acres. We were charmed not merely with its lakes, statues, and grand old trees, but with its natural features; and in particular with the lofty rocky brow from which you command an extensive prospect of rich plains stretching far away beneath you, with a glimpse of the ocean. Brooklyn itself has not the attractions of New York, though it has many excellent private buildings. Towards the wharves there is a throng of commercial activity, but much of the town is used as a residence for those who do business on the other side of the river, so that it is sometimes called the bed-room of New York.

I looked into Mr Beecher's church, and was surprised at its homely character. It is a plain brick edifice, without tower or spire of any kind, the front wall unrelieved by pillar or porch, and only broken by unornamental doors and windows. Above the gallery—which goes entirely round the church—there is a small extra one opposite the pulpit, which may accommodate about two hundred sitters. Otherwise it does not seem larger than our ordinary churches at home. And yet how widely known over the world is the preacher of this Tabernacle! And how soon, after I saw it, was that pulpit emptied for ever of him whose form and voice were, for forty years, so familiar there, and who occupied the foremost place among American orators! Mr Beecher died on the 8th of March, 1887. His name, associated with that of his gifted sister, will doubtless find a place in every faithful record of the early struggles for the freedom of the slave.

Not far from what must long continue to be know as Mr Beecher's church, is that of Dr. Talmage. It is also built of brick, but somewhat more ornamental outside, and to all appearance is larger than its neighbour.

There are several handsome public buildings in Brooklyn. The Town Hall is really a noble pile, and connected with it are all the arrangements required for self-government; as the city is an independent one, not in any sense under New York, and in size not very far from that of Glasgow. Having more space to grow than New York (which is confined to the area of a not very large island), Brooklyn is extending in various directions; and its streets are much more richly wooded, many of them appearing like lovely country avenues, shops and well-tenanted houses, from certain points of view, being almost entirely hidden behind the verdure. I had to return to it occasionally to visit friends from the old country. One of these visits was to a family who had formerly an ecclesiastical connection with us, and it was amusing, when looking for the house, where I expected to give a surprise, to hear one's name called out by a voice, adding, "This is the way." It was equally amusing to a friend who accompanied me, and who had long been in America, to hear the excellent old grandmother speak as if she had come straight not only from the land, but from the days of Burns.

The Brooklyn Bridge, along which we returned to New York, and by which we frequently afterwards crossed and re-crossed the river, was a source of increasing wonder and admiration. Its fine proportions made it most pleasing to look at—it seemed so graceful, light, and airy, with a span between the two towers of 1600 feet, yet able to bear a greater strain than any bridge of the kind in existence. On the Suspension Bridge at Menai Straits—a marvel in its way—a company of soldiers are forbidden to walk in step lest it should break under them. But here is a bridge of similar construction, on which are two lines of railway, with trains generally crowded with passengers, meeting each other midway, and leaving either extremity every few minutes; besides two waggon roads each 19 feet broad, where most ponderous vehicles are always on the move; and, rising above all, a footpath 15 feet wide. The Menai Bridge is only 1000 feet long and 100 feet above high water, whereas the Brooklyn Bridge is 5987 feet long, and the railway 135 feet above high water. We proceeded on the first occasion by the footpath, exalted above the other ways, and with a wide and unobstructed prospect all around; and we were tempted to linger long, resting on the seats provided under the shadow of the central tower, which rises to a height of 276 feet, or gazing over the parapet on the strange grand scene. A good way beneath us, on either side of the bridge, trains and waggons were rattling along; and far down was the yawning gulf of broad waters, where vessels were seen with their tall masts under our feet, and steamers glided through like little models. We had also New York and Brooklyn disclosing themselves in an extensive bird's-eye view, with the more distant Jersey City, and the broad harbour between, all full of life; while Sandy Hook and the distant highlands were faintly seen standing on a stripe of the quiet, far-off ocean. The works connected with this marvellous structure were thirteen years in progress, from 1870 to 1883, and cost upwards of three million pounds sterling. They were not, however, erected as a boast, but as a necessity, on account of the obstruction of floating ice on the river during some winters, when steam-ferries were exposed to great danger, and often delayed for hours in crossing.*

We had a delightful trip up the Hudson with a young friend (Mr J. Taylor) familiar with the scenes through which we passed. Steamboats go all the way to Albany, 145 miles from New York: our object, however, was West Point, about 53 miles up the river. It was considered late in the season, yet there were several hundreds on the pier waiting to go on board, with ample accommodation for hundreds more. These steamers are admirably adapted for their purpose and place, being scarcely boats, such as we call by that

---

* The Forth Bridge, at present in process of construction at Queensferry, and one of the greatest engineering wonders of our day, is 8091 feet long; its railway is 150 feet above high water; the three towers, known, in this peculiar kind of structure, as cantilevers, are 350 feet above the piers; and its two great spans are each 1710 feet. All these dimensions are largely in excess of those of the Brooklyn Bridge. The estimated expense of the Forth Bridge, however, is only £1,600,000, and the estimated time for construction is seven years; in both respects not much more than half those of the Brooklyn Bridge; but as the estimates were greatly exceeded by the reality in the American work, so most likely will it be in the Scottish. In regard simply to length, both of these bridges are excelled by that over the St. Lawrence at Montreal, which is 10,380 feet; and the new one over the Tay at Dundee, which is 10,612 feet. But none of these others can compare in graceful appearance with the Brooklyn Bridge, and none of them have its various conveniences for passengers, with the choice of going on foot, or by any kind of conveyance, besides the railway car.

name, but floating saloons, with no masts, and little, if any, shipping tackle. All is arranged for accommodation, comfort, and speed—which often reaches 24 miles an hour—nothing being required to enable them to face heavy seas, which are unknown in these sheltered waters. They have three decks, the engine protruding through the upper one, where a large crank is seen unprotected, rising in the air, and rolling to and fro in a rather curious fashion.

We could not forget, as we sailed up this noble river, that it was here, for the first time in the history of the world, that passengers were conveyed by steam. The idea had been taken from Scotland, where a steamboat had been used previously on the Forth and Clyde Canal to tow vessels. But a steamer conveyed passengers on the Hudson some five years before Bell put his *Comet* on the Clyde — the first on European waters. The American success, however, was accomplished by Fulton, himself a Scotchman. This association was pleasing, but not needed to make the voyage interesting, as it had many and varied natural charms peculiar to itself.

On the west bank of the river, for some fifteen miles, we passed crags of perpendicular rock, called the Palisades, columnar in structure, like the Giant's Causeway, and between four and five hundred feet high. They are not bare, however, as are those ocean-beat rocks which, in some respects, they resemble, but fringed with various forest trees, which were already taking on the first tints of autumn—the beautiful season known as the Indian summer. The wild vine, which climbs up the stems and branches of these trees, was particularly striking. The leaves were thoroughly influenced by the season, and appeared in brilliant fiery red, or like wreaths of gold, standing out in pleasing contrast with the prevailing green.

On the east bank the hills rose more gradually, but were also richly wooded, dotted with goodly villas, and having thriving ports, at most of which we called. The river at this part varied in breadth from one to two miles; but a little above, it opened to something like a lake, four miles broad, and continued thus for upwards of ten miles. The hills here began to rise higher, with lovely glens appearing now and again between. The scenery often reminded me of the Firth of Clyde, but more frequently of the Rhine; only destitute of the innumerable castellated ruins which adorn the ancient river, but amply compensating for this lack in having noble trees, with lofty rising ground, instead of scraggy vine-clad terraces.

About half way on our voyage we passed the spot where Washington Irving spent the last ten years of his life, where he liberally entertained his friends, edited a collective edition of his works, adding to them his lives of Goldsmith, Mahomet, and last of all, and most ap propriately, that of Washington; immediately on the completion of which he died, and was buried here in 1859. His house he called Sunnyside, but a village has sprung up since near by, which has been called after himself—Irvington.

Throughout our entire voyage the river was enlivened by crafts of all kind, yachts and sailing vessels often wending their way by tacking from side to side; besides steamers, tugs, and barges, some bent on pleasure, but most on business. The business aspect of the towns, with their various works, not always sightly or free from smoke, gave a different character to the scene from that to which we are accustomed on the estuary of the Clyde, but seldom marred the generally grand and pleasing effect.

At West Point we landed under bold cliffs, and climbed by a steep zig-zag road, at the top of which we found a broad plateau, on a promontory, where the river narrows. This commands a magnificent view far up the stream, including objects not only of natural but of historical interest. Just opposite is the house of the late Miss Susan Warner, better known by her *nom de plume* of Miss Wetherell, where her "Wide, Wide World," and most of her books— favourites with the ladies—were penned. Stretching across the river immediately below us, was placed the boom, or chain, which for long prevented the English frigates from proceeding further during the

Revolutionary War. About seven miles above, and in full view, is Newburgh, where Washington and his army were encamped for a year and a half; and where, when peace was ultimately proclaimed, the soldiers set those hill tops, some of them 1500 feet high, ablaze with bonfires; and where, with sad partings, the army was disbanded.

It is most appropriate, with such surroundings, that West Point should be chosen as the site of a great military college. It was itself a most important stronghold during the war, and might still be useful in resisting the passage upwards of any foe. But there were reasons much more to the purpose, and thoroughly practical, which led to the selection. It is admirably suited for training young soldiers, affording a fine situation for the numerous schools and homes for young officers and cadets, and ample scope for gun and drill practice. There is no town at hand with its various temptations, but wild highland hills with many a bold and rugged cliff, in scaling which they may strengthen their limbs, and develop their military skill. We only trust that the training here acquired will never result in the American people being induced to send forth the torch of war, but may enable them, as long as they retain their nationality, to bear the olive branch of peace triumphantly over the length and breadth of their great continent.

CHAPTER VI.

To the City of Penn.

FROM New York to Jersey City we had a short sail in order to reach the Pennsylvania Railway; or, as the Americans, according to their universal custom, would call it, rail*road*. Steam-ferries cross the Hudson—here about a mile broad—every few minutes. These are by no means handsome vessels, but spacious and comfortable, having large saloons on either side, capable of holding nearly a thousand passengers, and with a carriage way between, completely separate, where more than a dozen waggons, and other vehicles, or even an entire train, can be accommodated. There are upwards of thirty ferry-boats plying in various directions to and from the Jersey side. The city itself has few attractions, being chiefly a terminus for some of the greatest railroads in the country; though it has also some thriving wharves and manufactories of its own. The trains run in the middle of the principal streets, with parallel cart and carriage ways, all coming close together, separated only by a low, and scarcely visible, iron railing.

My destination, in the first instance, was Newark, to which I proceeded with a young friend, Mr. Robert Symington, whom I had known from his earliest days, and who had there formed a home of his own. The route presented nothing striking, except, perhaps, in the vast meadows and marshes, which, I understand, are fine breeding places for mosquitoes. And these creatures are sometimes striking enough. Their attentions, however, I wonderfully escaped, not only here, but during my entire stay in America; though I was told they were particularly fond of strangers, had sometimes heard their sharp buzz coming to a sudden termination as if they had just fastened on me, had seen some slain in the act of attacking a neighbour, and was shown a hand thickly studded with their marks a few days after they had been inflicted. I had no love for the curtains provided as a protection, looking on them as rather ominous, and just as likely to shut in a hungry mosquito with you—when he could find no other amusement than to prey upon you—as to shut him out from you.

Around Newark I found a beautiful district, well wooded, and varied by hill and dale. Arrangements had been kindly made for our driving at once through Orange and its neighbourhood, where we passed numerous charming country residences, chiefly the homes of New York merchants, who may travel daily to business, as the distance is only about twelve miles. The villas looked out smiling from the woods, above which, every now and again, church spires suddenly appeared pointing heavenward, giving a picturesque and settled Christian character to the whole scene.

Climbing up the slopes of the Orange mountains, we drove through Llewelyn Park, which has much natural and artifical beauty, and is finely laid out for building purposes, already largely taken advantage of. The ground has nothing of the level plain which we generally associate with the word park, but is hilly, almost mountainous, with endlessly varied undulations rising towards the lofty summit. The houses are completely isolated from each other, secluded and shaded by forest and ornamental trees; not hidden, however, behind walls or frowning fences, but with gardens and other surroundings exposed to view through pleasing openings in the woods. It seemed as if we were in private policies, on a visit to some lordly proprietor, instead of being in public grounds divided into numerous allotments. At times the way was rustic and homely, like a sequestered Scottish glen, till we reached the Eagle Rock, where we had an extensive prospect, not unlike that which is obtained from Richmond Hill, only seen here from a loftier elevation.

I spent a very pleasant evening with the family of my friend, and that of the Rev. Dr. Waters—though unfortunately he was himself from home at that time. In the morning we visited the church, which is in every respect a model of its kind. The class-rooms for Sabbath Schools and other purposes, with the splendid children's library, and every possible convenience for carrying on religious instruction, not to speak of the entrance halls, which resemble those into a noble mansion, cannot be excelled, even in New York. The organist, Mr. Ilsley, kindly came to show us the power of his instrument; but I was more anxious to witness his own power, as I knew of him before from his original pieces, one of which—"Driftwood,"—I had received some years ago, and enjoyed to hear at home. Referring to the completeness of the church, and all its means for carrying on Christian work, I asked if he could imagine anything awanting, when he replied, as the only thing he could think of, "An elevator for the organist."

I regretted to learn, shortly after returning to Scotland, that this accomplished, enthusiastic, and warm-hearted musician was called to his rest. He received a very cordial eulogy from the press of the city. Another gentleman, much more widely known, was also removed from Newark about the same time—Dr. Ray Palmer, the author of "My Faith looks up to Thee," and other pieces familiar at meetings, and in churches, throughout the Christian world. He resided here for many years, and an introduction to him was suggested by a mutual friend, but knowing his advanced years—about 80—and his infirm health, I did not accept of it. He died on the 29th March, 1887; and among the last words that escaped his lips, he was overheard repeating a verse of one of his own hymns:

> "When death these mortal eyes shall seal,
> And still this throbbing heart,
> The rending veil shall Thee reveal
> All glorious as Thou art."

I visited the thread mills of G. A. Clark & Brother, which are as extensive as those in Paisley, from which the Newark Works have sprung, and they are still making large additions. My attention was turned to some of the newest inventions and improvements, one or two of which especially interested me. There was a machine, just put to work, which, of its own accord, stopped the bobbin when the supply of thread on it was complete, made a slit in the wood, cut the thread and fixed it in the slit, and then tossed the bobbin into a box. There was another machine, also new, into which a long, and apparently endless ribbon of white paper passed, where it was printed with the trade mark in blue and gold, cut into circular portions, gummed, then neatly fastened on both ends of the bobbin, which was tossed into another box. The whole process, in both cases, was accomplished by iron fingers, and as rapidly performed as the account of it can be read. The rate was some 300 per minute. A gentleman from Florida, on seeing these novelties, humorously remarked that there were many men down South who had not the brains of one of these machines.

Mr. Clark, however, seeks to cultivate the brains of his workmen, as well as to employ their hands and introduce such mechanical helps. He has erected handsome buildings where are class-rooms for instruction in the evenings, a library and reading-room supplied with abundance of literature, and apartments for recreation and amusement. There is also a Savings' Bank connected with the mills, a Relief Society in case of sickness, an Athletic Society, a Rowing Club, and a Fire Brigade. This last, I understand, has done good service on several occasions.

Here we have surely a noble specimen of how they do these things in America. But we must not overlook the fact that the origin of these mills was in Paisley, where we have still the great parent works, in many respects a pattern in their way. It is so also with the thread-mills of the Messrs. Coats, which, like those of the Messrs. Clark, are represented on both sides of the Atlantic.

I had not time to visit the other extensive works in Newark, such as those for paper-making, and the Pennsylvania Railroad repairing works, where several thousand men are employed. I may notice that it was here celluloid was lately invented, an imitation of ivory and tortoise-shell, now most extensively used over the world; and here is still its home. The town itself is large and prosperous —about the size of Dundee—beautifully laid out in rectangular streets, lined with trees, and adorned with parks, one of which seemed to have very much the appearance of an old English village green. I left the town, pleased with its appearance, but especially with the fellowship enjoyed in the midst of kind and warm-hearted friends.

In the forenoon I proceeded to Princeton, one of the most celebrated seats of learning in America. It is about forty miles further west, and reached by a small branch from the main line. The country, most of the way, is well cultivated; though the brown of the Indian corn, and of the soil, where it may have been removed, contrasts unfavourably with our green fields at home; and I fear they have no "stubble butter." There is a pleasing relief, however, in the rich and varied forest trees, of which we never lose sight, most of them still in their summer freshness. The numerous College buildings, finely situated on a rising ground, stand out prominently as you approach them. The town, which is almost entirely dependent on the College, is, from this direction, hidden behind.

Armed with introductions, I called on President M'Cosh, when I was received, first by his excellent lady—the doctor not being in at the moment—and then by himself, in the most cordial manner; and by each in succession pressed to dine. Their daughter and her two children were present, forming a pleasing family party. We had a free conversation about the college, and books in general, which I need not repeat. But I may notice that, when asked by one of the ladies what I thought of Dr. Drummond's "Natural Law in the Spiritual World," I answered, in true Scotch fashion, by asking the President what *he* thought of it; when he replied that he had not read it. Strange enough for the author of "Typical Forms," and his earlier work, the "Method of the Divine Government," both so much in Dr. Drummond's line. His daughter, however, he said, had read it; and, from her account, he formed his own opinion regarding its main principle. He said there could not be that identity between the natural and spiritual world, which it was the purpose of the book to prove; and that analogy was a stronger argument for truth than even identity. This seems to be the prevailing view on both sides of the Atlantic; and yet in spite of this objection to the author's pet theory, the book is universally, and justly, admired for its culture, spirit, and graceful style; and the examples, in illustration of law, are cordially welcomed as furnishing excellent analogies.

We referred to the "New Princeton Review," in which the President said some ten thousand dollars had been invested, and which had then reached a circulation of about five thousand copies per number. A thousand more, however, he remarked, would be needful to make it safe, and completely successful. This, and more, we trust, it will soon receive, as from its genuine science, sound theology, and pure literature, it well deserves a place in every library, and in every study where these are valued.

The doctor's residence, which is comparatively new, is very spacious and handsome; a gift to the college—chiefly on his account—from the Stewarts of New York. It is on a most charming situation, commanding an extensive prospect. This the doctor was not unwilling to display. Throwing open the folding-windows in the drawing-room, and revealing, with evident pleasure, the lovely scene that stretched out before us, he asked if that did not resemble an English landscape. I acknowledged that it did; glad to find that here, as elsewhere, ours was the model, and that the highest compliment you can pay to an American landscape is to compare it to an English one.

The President, as is well known, is a Scotchman, though his light has long beamed from other shores. I referred to a visit he made some years ago to his native hills above Dalmellington, which I heard of from our minister in the neighbourhood, the Rev. James Patrick, of Patna, who had been greatly gratified by his preaching for him on that occasion. He said that few, if any, knew him there except by report. He is, however, still interested in Ayrshire, and familiar with many of its scenes, to which he kindly referred. Walking round the garden, rich in flowers and fruit, he pointed to an apple tree which had scattered its superabundance, saying, "what a grand catch that would be for the Troon boys." In the Princeton boys, too, he had evidently a kindly interest, speaking to them as we passed; asking what one was reading, and giving a word of commendation; and enquiring of others, who were going with measuring rod and chain, whether their work was for a special purpose or for practice. Age evidently has not made him cease to sympathize with youth.

We visited the various buildings connected with the college, now approaching a score, of which the doctor was most pardonably proud, as nearly the half of them were built in his time, and largely through his influence. The new chapel was just finished, and is a perfect gem, which would do credit to any in our large cities. Near it, standing apart, was a very chaste little building used for devotional meetings, the gift of a lady, in memory of a brother and sister who were drowned, regarding whom the President told me a touching story. I asked if the attendance at these meetings was optional. "Of course," he instantly replied. And yet there are three or four meetings there in a week, at which often 250 students are present. We afterwards passed the gymnasium, and I enquired if the attendance here was also optional, when the answer was as peremptory, "No, compulsory." Just so; you may compel safely in physical matters, but not in spiritual, else you crush out the spirit and leave merely the formal or the false. We looked into the astronomy classroom, where I was introduced to Dr. Young, the ablest spectroscopist in America, and successor to Dr. Mitchell, author of the popular work on "The Orbs of Heaven." I learned here, what I had not heard before, that the first telegraphic wire that conveyed a message did so across the courts of Princeton College. In the library, after pointing out some of the literary treasures, the President called my attention to the fine general effect of the room, and remarked that the late Dr. Tulloch, when there, pronounced it the most beautiful thing of the kind he had ever seen. In the museum—which is wonderful for its extent and variety, considering that it is in a comparatively new country—I was informed of an excellent scheme by which its geological department is replenished. Students who excel in this branch of study, as a reward, receive an appointment to visit certain districts and collect specimens, which they do, evidently, with zeal and skill; and the result is, the value of the museum is increased, and the knowledge of the physical structure of the States extended. I was much interested in having pointed out to me the house where Jonathan Edwards lived and died—a very homely structure compared with those which have risen around it since his day. The President's death was the result of inoculation, which he was induced to undergo on account of the prevalence of small-pox in the neighbourhood.

It was marvellous to see how Dr. M'Cosh, who is evidently above seventy years of age, tall, slender, and with pure silver locks, could walk from building to building, and mount stairs so nimbly, and at the end of fully an hour seem as fresh as ever. He had an engagement afterwards, but kindly ordered his trap, in which his daughter and her two children drove with me to the cemetery, situated a little way out of the village, where Jonathan Edwards, Aaron Burr, with the Presidents of the College, and several other men of mark, are buried. We then drove to the house of Dr. Paxton, who received me cordially, and called my attention to a spot behind it where Washington and his staff had once encamped; at the time, I suppose, when the battle was fought at Princeton, between the General and Lord Cornwallis. We also paid a visit to Dr. Archibald Hodge, which has now to me a melancholy interest. I referred to the place his late father's works occupy among our students, and in our ministers' libraries, and spoke also of his own writings. He was comparatively quiet, but looked healthy, with a fine ruddy countenance. What a surprise it was, therefore, to learn, from the public press on this side, that he had died on the 11th November last—some six weeks after I had seen him—and that Dr. Paxton conducted the funeral services at his grave! Thus, besides three in private life, I had met with two public men, during my stay on the other side of the Atlantic, who, shortly afterwards, passed into the eternal world. May we also be ready!

From Princeton to Philadelphia is a journey further west of about forty miles. I took this on a subsequent occasion, starting afresh from New York in the early morning, but may as well notice it in this connection. There was nothing specially interesting on the route except a brief glance into the cities of Elizabeth and New Brunswick, and crossing the broad waters of the Delaware at Trenton. This noble river, long familiar from its historic and poetic associations, was more or less in sight for twenty or thirty miles, as it flowed between wooded banks, above which vessels, in full sail, were seen gliding slowly along.

A favourable impression of Philadelphia — the Quaker city of Penn—was produced as we approached it in view of Fairmount Park and the Zoological Gardens, beautifully situated on the sloping banks of the Schuylkill river, between which and the Delaware the city lies. I did not proceed at once to the central terminus, but left at a station in the suburbs, as being nearer some friends whom I purposed first to visit. One of these, who lately left us to find a home with his children and grand-children, met me somewhat unexpectedly, when a little girl ran up and instantly leapt into my arms. She had been one of our Sabbath scholars a year or two ago, and would have been content here with a nod or a smile, but found there that "distance makes the heart grow fonder," and made all restraints vanish. Soon I was in the midst of three or four families whom I knew, or to whom I was known, hailing from Ayrshire. They were living side by side in the same street, and, I was gratified to learn, worshipped in the same church, at the door of which, on a Sabbath morning, some twenty or more of the clan frequently meet. I was gratified also to find representatives of this circle, and of others nearer at hand, who had been members of my congregation here, accidentally present when I preached in New York before returning home.

Philadelphia, not having her ordinary buildings so high as those of New York, with a smaller population, yet covers a larger area. But if her buildings generally are exceeded in height by those of other cities, she is resolved at least to have one grand edifice which will have no rival anywhere. I was not long in the neighbourhood till this attracted, if it did not absorb, attention. Some friends accompanied me from the suburbs, by New Market Street, which is fully eight miles long; and, for at least three of these, we had the great object of local ambition towering like a mountain before us. It is the City Hall, built at the point where Market and Broad Streets meet. Both of these streets being perfectly straight, as you approach the centre of the city by them, the entire height of the hall—fully 450 feet, and thus as high as the Pyramids of Egypt—is seen for miles, either from the north or the south, the east or the west. There are, indeed, few points within the compass of Philadelphia, and far beyond, where its silver summit does not command attention. The whole building is of pure white marble, and the cost, we were told, would largely exceed the estimate of ten million dollars. It is still in progress, and we saw large fluted columns, as they were being raised to ornament the top of the central tower, dangling far up in the air on ropes which seemed like threads, making one feel giddy to look at them, and alarmed lest some awful crash should be witnessed.

We passed along Chestnut and Walnut Streets; the most fashionable in the City, bright and lively with spacious shops and stores, after the manner of Buchanan Street or the Strand. We looked along Broad Street (not misnamed, as it is 113 feet wide), lined with splendid private residences and churches. But we lingered long at Independence Hall, the most interesting building, in many respects, I had yet seen in America. It has a very humble appearance, small and low-roofed, just as it was more than a hundred and fifty years ago. Near it Penn made his generous contract with the Indians; and beneath its roof the first Congress met, seeking to set matters right with this country, but ultimately constrained to declare the independence of the States, proclaimed on the steps where we stood, and rung in by the old bell now hanging silent in the lobby. Here is the room where the Constitution was framed, and where Congress continued to meet under its first President, and during the first twenty years of the history of the Republic, with its furniture unchanged, so that you can sit on the very seats occupied in those stirring times by Washington, Benjamin Franklin, and the like. We spent a short time in the museum, or curiosity room, next to that of Congress, trying to decipher autographic letters of these great heroes; and not even despising to look at the curious spectacles through which Washington often looked when he penned his weighty despatches and the farewell address which he delivered in the room above.

But I must leave the numerous attractions of the Quaker City, regretting that only one day could be given to them, and that only part of our experience there can be recorded. Our plans required that I should return at night to New York, to set out immediately for the North. We shall see more, however, of Pennsylvania, and have glimpses again of Philadelphia, as we pass to the West. Meanwhile we may look at Longfellow's description of the wooded land of Penn, and the city streets, around which the poet has thrown the charm of his genius.

> "In that delightful land which is washed by the Delaware's waters,
> Guarding in sylvan shades the name of Penn the apostle,
> Stands on the banks of its beautiful stream the city he founded.
> There all the air is balm, and the peach is the emblem of beauty,
> And the streets still re-echo the names of the trees of the forest,
> As if they fain would appease the Dryads whose haunts they molested."

CHAPTER VII.

To Niagara.

STARTED for Canada with my young travelling companion, and a gentleman from New York, Mr. Lindley, whom I had met with occasionally there, and who was going on business to Buffalo. The guidance, fellowship, and hospitality of this gentleman were of inestimable value. His native place was Natal, and having travelled much, and being remarkably intelligent, he had a fund of information which would have made any journey a joy. But he was specially familiar with this one, going over the ground —about 450 miles—frequently every year.

After crossing the Harlem river—really an arm of the sea, and, with the Hudson, making New York an island—we proceeded along the left bank of the Hudson, surveying from the land the same wooded cliffs and hills which we had previously seen from the water. Beyond West Point and Newburgh the scenery became tame, and there was nothing particular to attract us till we were upwards of a hundred miles from New York, when the Katskill range of mountains began to break the horizon with its bold, waving ridges. I thought I saw a patch of snow in a hollow far up toward the highest peak, but was told it was an hotel, which gradually developed its true character as we advanced. Another hotel could also be detected not far off, and both are said to be about 3000 feet above the river. The whole range, which is long and broad as well as lofty, is a favourite retreat from the glowing plains in summer, furnishing ample scope for the artist, the angler, and the hunter.

At Albany, our stay, at this time, was short, and my chief association with that visit was the linking of the dining-car to our train. This incident may have left its impression, partly on account of the welcome supplies which it brought, and partly because it furnished something of a novelty. The car, which was considerably larger than our carriages at home, was entirely devoted to culinary operations and to consuming their results. I was curious to inspect the kitchen, where, as we swept along at the rate of nearly forty miles an hour, roasts and stews, and all kinds of baked meats were being prepared by the lively coloured cooks; and where tables, capable of accommodating between thirty and forty persons, were tastefully spread as for *table d'hote* in a first-class hotel. Of course, my interest was not diminished when I was called to share the ample provision, nor marred in the least by this being served with hands as dark as those of the cooks. To assure us, I suppose, that colour—black as ink —was not inconsistent with cleanliness, both cooks and waiters were dressed in spotless white garments.

On American railways, passengers may walk from the extreme end of the train through all the carriages, passing over the couplings with perfect safety, if with care; and they often do so for a little exercise, or to see if they have any friends "on board," to have a chat with them, or to get a hearty and hot meal direct from the kitchen. In some cases, as I found in the Pennsylvania line— and I suppose it is the same generally—you may order what you want to be brought to your own carriage, when a board is fixed opposite your seat, where you can dine, lunch, or take tea, alone; or, by turning the seat before you on its pivot, you can reverse it, making the back become the front, and thus you may enjoy your meal at a little table, face to face with two or three friends. In all express trains, carriages are provided with every other convenience, such as comfortable dressing-rooms and smoking-room, iced-water to cool you in summer, and a stove to warm you in winter. There is also a somewhat ominous provision in the form of picks, axes, saws, and crow-bars, by which you may assist to dig yourself out of the debris, or cut your way through your carriage, when some awful smash has taken place.

We made few calls on our way North, as we had to reach Buffalo within twelve hours. Some of the towns at which we stopped were not very attractive; though there were those which bore such charmed names as Troy, Rome, and Syracuse. This last is four times larger than its ancient and insular namesake. But, whilst far from the sea, it is yet richly supplied with salt, the manufacture of which is its chief occupation. On this account it is surrounded by grim grey fields, with endless and unsightly wooden sheds used for drying purposes. It is rather a handsome town, we believe, in some portions, but as seen from the railway, it has few attractions. If not everywhere beautiful, however, it is wealthy, and worth its salt; which, in this case, means much, as supplies of the indispensable seasoning appear to be inexhaustible; seams of rock-salt having been wrought seventy feet thick, and we learned as we passed, that one had just been opened a hundred feet thick.

I was struck with the little care taken, in many cases, to protect the inhabitants of these towns, and of those in America generally, from railway accidents. The trains often pass through the streets, exactly as a horse-car does in our cities; children playing on the pavement, or even on the streets, within arm's length of the wheels. I knew of a case where a father and son, originally from Troon, residing in a town thus unprotected, in a moment of forgetfulness, crossed the street as a train was passing, and both were cut in pieces. I asked our friend if the Company would not be responsible for accidents: but he said he believed they would not, for the railway was first in the field, as is the case in many other districts, and the town, for convenience, put itself close beside it, and was thus bound to make a fence or take the consequences.

I was puzzled at first with the ringing of innumerable bells, as a train entered a town or village, and ran through its streets, or approached or left a station. At length, however, I discovered that the sounds proceeded from the engines at the head of every train, whose stokers were each pulling a rope attached to a bell, not to invite any in, but to ward all off. This contrivance, I should say, from my experience, is universal in such circumstances; and it is certainly a much more pleasant one than that of the horrid whistle, which is seldom heard in the States, except in extreme cases. But it may be questioned if the harmonious sound should be so much trusted as it is without any other safeguards.

During a good portion of our journey we went through the Mohawk valley; pleased to find an original Indian name, though all trace of the Indian tribe has long since vanished. On the sloping, and sometimes beautifully undulating banks of the river, were farm-houses and waving corn-fields, with villages and wooded dells. Almost constantly within view, parallel with us and the river, was a Canal, which joins Lake Erie with the Hudson, and then, by New York, joins it with the ocean.

Between Lyons and Rochester we swept past Palmyra, a town bearing a very ancient and honoured name, but associated, in this case, with one of the most degraded superstitions of modern times. It was on a hill side near this place that Joe Smith, who had resided here in his boyhood, declared that he made the discovery of the golden plates on which Mormonism is founded. Strange that what was really a discarded work of fiction could be so gilded over by fraud as to pass for a Divine revelation, and that this spot should be memorable as the source of a pollution which has become such a curse in one of the States, and is at present seriously taxing the wisdom and power of all the rest to remove.

It was dark before we reached Buffalo. Our notions of this town had been very hazy, and our chief association with it was its "green," which we long supposed to be that of a village, where "the gals came out at nights to dance." But we found that now, at all events, this exercise may be enjoyed on the lawns of a series of public parks containing some 530 acres, and be engaged in by some forty thousand boys and girls, both young and old. Our friend having secured for us most comfortable, nay spacious, quarters for the night, we were soon in the heart of the busy city, its streets and shops and squares all brilliant under the blaze of electric lights. There are five beautifully wooded squares, at some of which we observed, what we afterwards found to be common elsewhere, erections, composed of iron rods, forming tall, slender pyramids, rising above the buildings around, with a light like a little moon, sending its silver beams far and wide. I was amused at an American notion, which I observed in the morning under the window of our hotel, in the shape of a street car, off the rails, without horse or wheels, as if it had broken down, and which I learned was used as a waiting-room where passengers might find shelter till the moving cars, which passed by it, should arrive.

Our stay in Buffalo was chiefly as a stage by which we might reach the Falls, and see the Niagara River in daylight. I cannot sympathise with Mr. Froude when he tells us, in his *Oceana*, on occasion of his visit to Buffalo about a year and a-half ago, that he would not turn aside to see the Falls: and that he had treated them in the same manner on a former visit, when equally near them. As one reason for not going, he mentions that the rocks are painted with gigantic advertisements: but if he had gone he would have found that these no longer exist. As another reason, he quotes, what he considered the wise remark of his host to a gentleman who had expressed his wonder at "so vast a body of water falling over such a precipice." "Why is it wonderful that water should fall? The wonder would be if it did *not* fall." For such reasons, and "because much nonsense had been said about it," Mr. Froude, the historian of England, and biographer of Carlyle, would not go twenty miles out of his way to see the grandest phenomenon of its kind in nature. Surely all this is small on the part of a great man. Could it be that he would not condescend to go where the multitude went? We went, and the whole scene and surroundings will be a valued memory for life.

With the early morning we gazed on the unbounded waters of Lake Erie—the first of the chain of American fresh-water seas we had beheld—and were struck with the basins and piers on its shores, showing the extensive business it brought to Buffalo. But the railway ride along the Niagara River, which receives the overflow of all the great lakes above, was still more interesting. The river varies in breadth from one to three miles, and the current varies from two miles an hour at first, to a more gentle flow as the water widens, and then rapidly narrows as signs begin of the sweeping cataracts being near. It bears on its bosom vessels of all sizes, propelled by the oar or the sail, with steamboats plying to several pleasant little towns on both banks. These crafts often proceed far down, as if altogether heedless of the awful doom that awaited them if they ventured only a little further.

We had a short stay at Niagara village, during which our friend made a call, and we accompanied him. In the garden we plucked a few grapes, sweet and refreshing, as they grew unsheltered on the wall; but seeing the gardener crush a snake by our side, we felt it was at least one comfort that our humble gooseberry was free from such lively accompaniments. The small purple grapes, which grow in the open air in nearly all the States, are great favourites, appearing at almost every meal, sometimes interspersed with sparkling ice; but those of Niagara are held in highest esteem, perhaps on account of the constant supply of moisture they may receive from the spray of the Falls. The main street of the village presented us with a novelty, always looked at with curiosity for the first time by a stranger, in the shape of a "flitting," not of furniture, but of house and all. There were, in fact, two flittings, one building appearing in the middle of the street, and another in process of being lifted from its site, both two storeys high; but whether or not the dwellers were within we could not say, as the blinds were drawn.

Our invaluable friend wisely arranged that we should take a carriage part of the way, and walk at other parts, that we might see the Falls to the utmost advantage. We drove first to Prospect Point, when we came suddenly on the Fall on the American side, just where the great body of water bends over the precipice, at first almost in a solid mass, but immediately, breaking and foaming, plunges into the abyss, a depth from the surface of the river of 164 feet. The noise was terrific, drowning every other sound; and we were only protected from the torrent by a little wall built round the edge of the rock that overlooks it. A pic-nic party visited this spot several years ago, and a lovely little girl, the life and joy of the company, was lifted up in sport by a gentleman—her special favourite—and held over the rushing flood, when, losing command of himself, he let her drop, and no trace of her was ever afterwards found. I heard the late Mr. Gough tell the story with great effect in illustration of the danger of tampering with temptation.

Obtaining our first impressions from this point may have prevented the disappointment which is said to be felt by some when they first come on Niagara. Here we looked along a fall about eleven hundred feet broad; and right up to that of the Horse Shoe, stretching between the American and the Canadian sides for upwards of a thousand feet. The whole scene was thus brought into view at a glance, and as we gazed upon it, with the spray rising in a mass, thick beneath, but thinning and tapering above like the mane of some monster, its grandeur grew upon us; though, in the absence of sunshine, the rainbow tints were awanting.

We next drove through Prospect Park, where all troublesome tolls and unsightly advertisements have been removed, and the whole is being beautifully laid out for the public. Here, from a pleasing height, we surveyed the wide landscape of foaming waters, and gazed into the dark steep gorge which holds within its impregnable barriers innumerable contending eddies and whirlpools. We descended by an elevator to a point on the brink of the river almost immediately below the American Fall, and looked up on the flood which we had witnessed from above; but a slight wind sent the spray on us in such quantities that we had to make a hasty retreat, pushing up umbrellas and scrambling over the rocks with much difficulty, if not with danger. Had the fall bent more fully toward us, how ludicrous, as well as alarming, our situation would have been, seeking to ward off the overwhelming torrent by an umbrella, as Mrs. Partington endeavoured to sweep the rising Atlantic from her house with a broom! A small steamer, called the *Maid of the Mist*, is now plying across the river from this point, and also goes up as near as possible to the foot of the Horse Shoe fall; but my young travelling companion was satisfied with the misty experience from the shore, without seeking it again from the water.

A little above the American Fall we crossed the

cataracts by an iron bridge, the erection of which, on rocks covered with the torrent, seemed truly marvellous. It is an impressive sight to look from this bridge on the river rushing, almost at your feet, over the rugged bed, and dashing itself against every obstruction, unconscious of the awful plunge immediately before it. And is it not so with many in their career of guilt and crime, if conscious, equally heedless of the dreadful doom to which they are madly hastening? "Thou carriest them away as with a flood; they are as a sleep."

By this bridge we reached Goat Island, which divides the river into the two great falls, and is of itself of considerable extent and beauty. Then we passed on to what are called the Three Sisters, rocky wooded islands, divided by minor cataracts, and joined together by small iron bridges. From the furthest of these islands, holding on by an iron rod, we proceeded some distance literally on the torrent; touching the waters and tasting of them just as they were about to plunge over the Great Horse Shoe Fall, whose broken crest was fully before us, and whose roar was filling our ears. One could not stand here, looking on that awful commotion, and listening to that mighty sound, without realizing how appropriate was the name *Niagara*—thunder of waters—and thinking of Him to whom all was but a drop in the bucket: "The thunder of His power who can know it?" Yet we felt, at the same time, that there was a certain joy, as well as solemn majesty, in the whole, which gave a deeper meaning to the description, "His voice was as the sound of many waters."

We returned to Niagara village through Goat Island, by woods and dales, which afforded glimpses, now and again, of the grand scenes whose sound was never absent. The Government of the United States is evidently anxious to bring back the neighbourhood to something like its original grandeur and beauty, by destroying all buildings, or unsightly objects, which may have marred it. A mill stood close to the bridge which crosses the cataracts, but we saw workmen busy removing its foundations—apparently at no small risk—so that now, or soon, nothing will be seen all around to offend the eye or distract the attention. Large portions of land also are being purchased in several directions within sight of the Falls, drives and walks opened up, disclosing charming views, and plans laid down for an International Park—that is, grounds not the property of any one State, but of the nation as a whole.

We left the American side, and with it the great Republic, by the Suspension Bridge, on the middle of which we paused for a minute to gaze on, or, as we might say, to drink in, the wild scene of troubled waters from a favourite point of view. In another minute we were in Canada, and on British soil. Nor were we allowed to forget this, as the Union Jack was waving in the breeze. Our generous American friend was left on the other side, but not our gratitude to him; nor our love for his great country, which we had already learned to honour as we had never done merely by report. Still, we are loyal British subjects, and our hearts were stirred by the sight of

> "The flag that braved a thousand years
> The battle and the breeze,"

giving us a sign of the protection we could here claim as a right; and a home feeling, though the place of our nativity was as far away as ever.

A run along the river, up to and beyond the Canadian Fall, and among the various islands formed by the cataracts there, with a look into the *burning spring*—dark and cold when we saw it—were soon accomplished. The petty tolls and taxes here exacted seem unworthy of the nation; and we were vexed to think that our own people should be behind those of the United States in sweeping such nuisances away. Our last sight of the river was near the railway bridge, immediately above which we looked across that part which Captain Webb attempted to swim, and in which he perished. Some distance below is the whirlpool which has been passed, once or twice lately, by the cooper in his *cask*, thus degrading it, as some say, into a mere *cascade*.

Around Niagara we had lingered from early morn till dewy eve. Nor did we grudge the time, conscious that we had not done it more than justice.

A gentleman told me he had been there for a month, at the close of which one of the guides, who had often offered his services in vain, assured him there was something he had not seen, and which he was willing to show without fee. The agreement was made, and our friend was taken to the American Fall, asked to turn his back on it, then lie on the rocks, and, from this prostrate position, look upwards on the descending floods. He did so, and confessed that he certainly obtained a new and most impressive sight. We were satisfied, however, with the view we already had, in perpendicular position, from the same spot, where we required all the freedom of our limbs to escape the drenching waters; and we were content to turn our backs on Niagara, as a whole, grateful for what we had beheld, and looking forward to new, if not to nobler, scenes.

CHAPTER VIII.

To Montreal.

FROM Niagara we were booked for Toronto, from which we expected to go by boat, the following afternoon, on Lake Ontario to the river St. Lawrence. But we turned aside to spend the evening at Galt, which is situated among the hills, a little to the west of Hamilton. There was no scenery at first to charm us by the way; and perhaps it was well, as it might have had but scant justice, after what we had seen. It was unfortunate, however, that just as we were entering among the hills, a veil was being thrown over them, for "the shades of night were falling fast."

We were not conscious of any change of climate —though we had gone pretty far north in the course of two days—nor did we feel any chill from the evening air. But the Canadians, in spite of their being accustomed to the severest cold, seem either to dread its approach, or lose no time in putting themselves on the defensive; for already, on the 28th of September, the stove was glowing in the car. It was too much for us to be near it, and, for our comfort, we had to keep at a respectful distance.

When we reached Galt the darkness was dense, and as we had only the evening hours to spare, and were anxious to visit a family at one time connected with Troon, we were glad to obtain the guidance of a young man, who, in more ways than one, was a most valuable aid. There was not a lamp to show us whether we were on a road or in a field, whether we were approaching a bridge, or going right into the stream, whose rush we heard near us. We had literally to walk the plank, or, to speak more accurately, two or three planks, which formed the pavement. This, we found afterwards, was common in Canada, only in the larger towns the number of planks is increased. The highway was avoided in the dark; for, as we suspected, it was only an earth road—that is, one that has not yet been disturbed by the sons of Macadam. We had driven occasionally along such roads in the States, where, even in broad daylight, it was something of a feat, resembling a row in a small boat during a ground swell; but for strangers like ourselves, to walk there in a moonless night without lamps, was certain to make us reel to and fro, and might result in something very unseemly, if not unsafe. We did not expect the splendours of the electric light, but we think the good people of this fine thriving little town, with several public works, and, I suppose, several thousands of a population, might supply gas, or at least oil, to enlighten visitors, and brighten their own paths by night, in harmony with their bright and beautiful surroundings by day. The reason our guide gave us for this neglect was that most of their local officials were Scotchmen, and very careful.*

We found the friends we sought, and received a cordial welcome, but regretted to see the mother laid aside by long sickness. Before we parted, the children, with parents and grandchildren, were gathered together in the sick chamber, and we had worship, such as we were accustomed to have, long ago, in their Scottish home. Seeing us off with the early

---

* A correspondent from Galt, vexed at the brevity of our visit, and at our benighted experience, has since informed me that gas pipes were being laid, and lamp posts being fitted up, even when I was there; that the streets are now well lit, that the churches are equally privileged, and that some of the stores and public works have the benefit of the electric light. I am also told that, among other works, there are eight foundries and machine shops; two edge-tool works; various mills for grinding corn and wheat, and manufacturing woollen cloth; factories for making gloves, and felt, and files, and wheels; and a pin manufactory, producing a million and a-half per day. The town also has provided for itself three Presbyterian Churches, containing some 2700 sittings amongst them; one Methodist Church, one Baptist, one Episcopalian, one Roman Catholic, a Salvation Army Hall, three public schools, a Collegiate Institute with students from all parts, and two weekly papers. Surely this is well for a town with a population of some seven thousand! Although little known on this side of the Atlantic, it is distinguished on the other side as the Manchester of Canada; and it would have been a pity if we had not learned what the daylight, and a little more time and examination, would have disclosed. Perhaps this may suffice as an illustration of the fact that, in a holiday visit, ample justice cannot be done to details in any place, and that, even of what we heard, in several instances "the half has not been told."

morning, the father furnished us with several photographs of his family, among which was that of a son who had built a small steamboat on the river that passes through the town, but which, on its first trip, refused to answer the helm, or was not properly steered, and instead of going up, went down the stream, and was precipitated over a water fall, where many were killed or drowned, and our young friend among them. Shortly after returning to Scotland, I learned that the sick mother had gone to her rest.

Leaving Galt, we had to wait for a little at a junction, as had also a large gathering proceeding westward to London, with instrumental bands accompanying them. It was pleasing to see the good humour and kindly familiarity manifest by the crowd, reminding us of similar scenes in many a rural district in Scotland, from which a large portion of the people evidently sprung. We had again to pass through Hamilton, a busy city, thriving by the trade on the Lake and surrounding country; and the earnest contentions at the station for the sale of the morning papers clearly showed that, in the news department at least, it was fully up to the times. The population is now forty thousand—double that of its Lanarkshire namesake.

Our ride from this continued along the shores of Lake Ontario, where, now and again, we dipped into woods, or crossed little creeks, by bridges or piles, obtaining glimpses of the great waters. Leaving the train at Toronto, we were received by a young man who at once recognised us, though it must be nearly fifteen years since we saw him. He was the son of our friend at Galt, and a message had been sent by telephone of our coming, so that he was ready to welcome us. It was still early in the day, and he devoted nearly all the remainder of it to show us the town, his friends, and his hospitality. We were much pleased with the general appearance of Toronto, though it has little to boast of in the way of scenery, being situated on a flat bank of the Lake, with nothing very prominent in the neighbourhood. It has a population of 130,000, thus fully larger than Aberdeen; and a great part of it is well built of stone and finely coloured brick, with excellent shops and public buildings, including the University —one of the finest buildings of the kind in America— the new Court House, and numerous handsome Churches.

We met with a disappointment at Toronto. Immediately before reaching the station, a person entered with what seemed a huge supply of keys, like those of a jailor, hanging over his arms and shoulders. This was the baggage clerk, with his thongs and checks. We gave him our bag, round which he placed his thong giving us the corresponding check, and promising that our bag would be put on board the steamboat for Kingston and Montreal. In due time in the afternoon we arrived at the pier, but neither the boat nor the baggage was there. The steamer had not arrived from Kingston that morning, having been put back by a fierce storm on the Lake. It may seem strange to be thus baffled by an inland gale. But though these boats are large and powerful, as some we saw at the pier going elsewhere, yet with such a wind as blew that morning from the west, having a reach of fully two hundred miles of water, it is not wonderful that they sometimes fail. Better, perhaps, that we did not know this by experience, as it would have been a disgrace, after crossing the ocean in comfort, to have been driven back on a lake with fresh water sickness. By telephonic communication from the office our bag was discovered, and promise given that it would appear at the railway station at the hour of our starting, as we had resolved to go by train. And punctually it turned up accordingly, proving all the more, through this mishap, the perfection of the American baggage system.

We had three or four more hours to spare in Toronto than we expected, and had an opportunity of visiting the east or south-east end of the city, which we found inferior to the west; the houses being chiefly of wood, one of which we saw in process of being raised a few feet higher over the same site, while the inmates were apparently going about their usual occupations within.

To improve the time still at our disposal, and make up somewhat for our disappointment in losing the long sail on the Lake, we resolved to have a row on it in a small boat. In response to our enquiries at a person likely to have such things at his disposal, we were surprised to be taken into his well filled boat-house, and see the objects of our ambition stowed away on shelves, tier above tier, like hat-boxes in a shop. We were also amused to see him select one for us, lift it in his arms and carry it as easily and gently as if it had been a child, and then lay it tenderly into the water at the point of a wooden pier.

It might be thought a deed of fool-hardiness to venture, in any craft, on these waters on the very day that a powerful steamer could not face them. But what can be said of going there and then in such a coracle? Simply that it furnished a fine illustration of the difference which time and place make on these inland seas. The winds had already suddenly subsided, and every trace of the storm had gone; so that, though our boat could not safely hold more than two—including crew and passengers—and would require cautious handling in any circumstances, yet we were able easily and safely to paddle it along. There was only the ripple of comparatively tiny waves, which seemed to smile in the soft light, and to clap their little hands on the slender boards beneath us, rejoicing over the return of peace. Of course, something of this was due to the fact that we were on the lee-side of the Lake, but much also is characteristic of its waters. Well if our wrath was like theirs, thus speedily vanishing, the sun not allowed to go down upon it!

We rowed toward a lovely island about a mile and a-half from the shore. This is a favourite resort with the inhabitants of Toronto; so near them, and yet furnishing a fine contrast to the crowded streets of the city, with pleasing prospects and healthful breezes from the Lake. Besides two or three hotels, it has a sanitorium, erected by some benevolent citizens, for sick children. It is also the home of many a splendid yacht, and the starting point for many a keenly contested race. One or two of these yachts passed us, looking most swan-like, and making graceful progress with the breath of the evening breeze. We did not land, however,

"On' the island, green and grassy,
 Yonder on the Big-Sea Water,"

but lingered on the Lake, surveying the city, with its roofs and spires sparkling in the sunset, and watching the brilliant orb disappear behind the woods; while the whole scene glowed with beauty, and the Lake appeared "like a sea of glass mingled with fire."

We again visited the city, bright with its own lights; shops and lamps, and electricity everywhere, furnishing a fair equivalent for the departed day, and giving it a more lively appearance than is presented by many cities in the old country claiming greater wealth and progress. Altogether Toronto left a very favourable impression on us; and though it may have some things in which it differs from, or excels, it has still more in which it closely resembles a prosperous town in Scotland. In many respects it reminded me of home, as the Scotch element appeared very manifest in its streets, its people, and its dwellings. I was glad to learn especially that, in its religious spirit, loyalty to the truth, and love of the Day of Rest, it is not behind us. It has some eighty-five churches of all denominations, including sixteen Presbyterian. There are three colleges and two medical schools, none of them insignificant; also three Theological halls, where students of no mean culture are being trained, and from which preachers of the gospel are sent forth to labour over the length and breadth of the Dominion, as well as to lift up the standard in distant lands. Ministers from the old country are welcomed who may go out to their aid, but they must not be failures at home, but men of ability and Christian zeal, with the spirit of those educated on the spot, willing to endure hardness; for they will often have to travel far to meet the wants of scattered populations, sometimes " mid snow and ice."

After our pleasing experience at Toronto, we were so far satisfied to proceed by rail, and in the dark, along the northern shores of the Lake to

Montreal. Even though we had gone by boat we would have had a night on the water, when the greater part of the land would have been no less a blank. The morning dawned as we approached the St. Lawrence, just where it begins to be formed into a river emerging from the Lake, and we had occasional views of lovely islands—part of the famous Thousand—of varied forms and size, bright and smiling under the rays of the rising sun. We saw enough to make us grateful, and at the same time regret our loss in not being able to sail among them.

When we reached Montreal, having telegraphed that we were coming by rail, we were immediately recognised by a Canadian Captain, who had once kindly called on us on our own shores, and then by a goodly group of relatives, most of whom we had never seen before, but whom those who witnessed our greeting would suppose we had known all our lives. At this time we passed through the entire length of the City, which presented, in the west and centre, a scene of lively activity, with business premises and public buildings that would do credit to any city; but towards the east degenerated into monotonous shops of an inferior class, with unmistakeable *signs* of their French origin in the names above the doors — about one-half of the population of Montreal are of this nationality. Some of the streets, even the most busy and important, being comparatively narrow, there is only a single line for the tram-car; and this we often found an inconvenience, as we had to be shunted at certain points, waiting till the car coming in the opposite direction should pass.

Our head-quarters were not to be in the city— though we had frequently to visit it — but on the other side of the St. Lawrence, at Longueuil, which we reached by steam ferry. This town, or village, is French in its origin, and still chiefly French in its population. But there are several English and Scotch families, though now thoroughly Canadian, residing in it, either during the summer or permanently, whose business is in the city. Railway communication is maintained with this, and all the south side of the river, and on to the States, by the Victoria Tubular Bridge, a noble — in fact, a marvellous — structure, about two miles long, with strong massive piers to stem a powerful current of water, or a dreadful flow of ice. The steam-ferry, however, is more convenient for Longueuil in summer; and in winter the river is frozen, forming "the ice bridge," by which the people can cross to business—first on foot, and afterwards, if they will, by carriages or waggons, or even by trains; for rails are often laid on the ice, along which traffic to any extent can be conducted. But the breaking up in spring has its dangers, when the masses of ice and overflowing water which have been jammed in, set free, cut up the shore, injure the gardens, and occasionally flood the houses — the city itself also sharing in these calamities. Last spring (1887) was more than usually destructive in this respect, several miles of country and town being laid under water, and boats enabled and requiring to sail from house to house to save property and persons. Yet all this, I was told, might be prevented, or mitigated, if the authorities of Montreal would only be at the expense of blasting some rocks in the river.

The Canadian winter is what we would call very severe. The thermometer is sometimes 40 degs. below zero, just as in summer it is sometimes 100 degs. above it. But we were assured that it was looked forward to generally with pleasure as a delightful season. The clear, calm, dry atmosphere makes it most exhilarating and healthful. And those who cannot work during the long frosts, or otherwise have leisure, find many means of enjoyment and recreation, which prevent the time hanging heavy on their hands. Skating, of course, is an exercise in which the Canadians excel. But they also move rapidly on the ice in boats fitted with sails. They drive on the snow, through town and country, with their sleighs; or compete in the race with their shoes. They take to tobogganing, sitting on thin planks, formed like enormous skates, and sweep down steep hillsides with the swiftness of a swallow. When there are no natural heights for this exercise they form artificial ones, raising lofty wooden inclines, by which they obtain an impetus that sends them far along the surface of the snowy plain—although I did not think these structures very ornamental when left to stand, as they generally are, over the summer. Then there is above all a truly royal recreation in the building of Ice Palaces after the model of some of our baronial castles. These are often four or five stories high, manned, or ornamented in peculiar fashion, by more than a hundred men, and mock sieges are conducted when the ice sparkles under the brilliant fire works as if studded with millions of diamonds. The pictures of these palaces which come to us occasionally, slightly coloured, show that they are really handsome structures. And no wonder they draw crowds of visitors to Montreal from the States, as well as from various parts of Canada, especially during the time that the carnivals and festivities are carried on within and around them. Pity that the first thaw makes every pinnacle drop in tears, presaging total destruction in a few weeks! We saw the site, in one of the great squares of the city, where the lofty battlements so lately had proudly looked to heaven, and not a trace could be found. But such is pleasure, like the ice-palace, or

> " Like the snowfalls in the river,
>   A moment white—then melts for ever."

Our friendly shelter at Longueuil was a fair and

genuine specimen of a Canadian country cottage. It is built of wood, with its little verandah overlooking the shipping that passes to and fro from the great seat of commerce on the opposite bank of the St. Lawrence. We watched with interest the large steamers of the Allan line, which we had often seen on the Clyde, steadily approaching the port for which they had crossed the ocean, or starting on their homeward bound voyage. But we were still more charmed with the fellowship, and comforts, and curiosities within. The kitchen, especially, was a novelty, with its large stove in the middle of the floor, having most ingenious appliances for all kinds of cooking, and an important source of defence against the cold. The lively, thrifty housewife loves it as a friend, and fully expounded its varied qualities and excellencies; though I fear much of this was lost on our dull comprehension, which would certainly be discovered if we ventured to repeat it. We could easily understand, however, what a vast advantage it would be in winter, even for heating purposes; all the more that its flue was not led, as with us, at once outside to have its virtues soon lost, but passed inside the kitchen to the wall, then to the room above, where some of its genial influence might also be felt. Other stoves, which did not combine the cooking power, with pipes similarly led, were ready for use when the winter appeared.

One of the most delightful views of Montreal,

where we also had the best idea of its surroundings, was obtained from Mont Real—that is the Royal Mountain—which gives the City its name. By the way, before ascending it, I called on a gentleman to enquire after the Rev. G. Copland of Ayr, whom I hoped to meet here, saying, that, if he arrived, he might find us on the hill. "Beg your pardon," was the reply, "the mountain." Of course we smiled at the correction, as certainly we would not call a height of 750 feet a mountain. The good people of Montreal, however, do not merely call it so, but must think its ascent a serious undertaking, for they have provided a cable elevator, with an almost perpendicular ascent, to help them up part of the way. We sought to excuse ourselves for taking advantage of this unromantic aid to climbing, by the presence of a number of the fair sex in our company. But we must confess that, sitting in an easy chair, by which we were raised from the woods to the front of an open precipice, when a magnificent prospect suddenly burst upon us, was a luxury in the way of sight-seeing not to be despised. There was climbing to do afterwards to reach the summit; and to go higher still, for there is a lofty erection by which you may rise above the woods that crown the height, and have an unbroken sweep, for many miles around, of hill and dale, and broad rolling river, with the city lying at your feet; its streets and squares, and long lines of handsome villas, and spacious residences, with lofty church spires and towers and domes, and public buildings, and distant shipping, all giving token of wealth, and taste and prosperity. Around the mount there is a circuit of nine miles, with numerous walks and varied views in every direction, the whole free to the public—in fact public property. It was touching to see two cemeteries—the Protestant and the Roman Catholic—in hollows about half-way up, nestling among trees which seemed to be growing in their natural state in the midst of the tombs.

There are numerous other walks and drives in this neighbourhood, and all around Montreal, together with sails on the Ottawa, and on the St. Lawrence with its little green islands, and round the great island on which the city is situated. During one of these sails I met with a gentleman from the States who remarked that it was an excellent place to spend a few days, as one could get his time "right squared up." This, I may notice, was about the only kind of slang which I heard during my tour, and on the whole it was not very objectionable, besides being in the circumstances very appropriate.

On descending from Mont Real I was much gratified with a visit paid to M'Gill College, which is situated at its base. The college consists of a fine range of buildings, comparatively new, in front of which is a park tastefully laid out, and with sufficient scope for games. We inspected the class-rooms, library, dormitories, and other apartments, all fresh and in excellent condition. We found many of the students in their private rooms, busy at their desks, with their little libraries before them, preparing their lessons for the following day. They all seemed comfortable and happy, and gave us a kindly greeting as we looked in upon them. I regretted, however, that I had not an introduction to Sir William Dawson—the Principal—whose works on science from a religious point of view are so well known in this country, as well as in America, and who had the honour of being called to preside at the meeting of the British Association, in September, 1886. His opening address had just been delivered, and printed in the newspapers, as we set sail from Liverpool. Its subject was "The Bed of the Atlantic," and doubtless, on that account, read with all the greater interest when we were on its bosom.

I visited the family of Dr. Wilkes, with a mutual friend, but was unfortunate in not finding the aged pastor at home. It would have been gratifying to have met with one, who, after reaching his eightieth year, crossed the Atlantic, and had just returned, welcomed by the people of Montreal, and the whole public press of the city, in a most cordial manner, and who has since received the warmer welcome to a better home. I found the announcement of his death, with other sad ones, shortly after I re-crossed the ocean.

May I be here permitted to say that in this

city I had numerous glimpses into private life, and received many a kindly reception from those who had hitherto been strangers to me, as well as from relatives, discovering unexpected links of connection with friends at home, which, with the early bite of the north wind, made it difficult to realise that I was not in Scotland?

CHAPTER IX.

To Quebec.

AD we sailed down the St. Lawrence, from Lake Ontario to Montreal, we would not only have seen the Thousand Islands, but we would have required to shoot the Rapids. Missing these latter was one of our chief disappointments in being deprived of the voyage. I was glad, however, to learn that the most interesting, though the shortest of these—known as the Lachine Rapids—were only about nine miles from Montreal, and that it was possible, by an early start, to catch the steam-boat a little above that point, and thus have an opportunity of seeing this remarkable feature of the river, and of enjoying the novel experience.

With a young friend, familiar with the route, I set out in the early morning, crossing to Montreal, and proceeding by train to Bonaventure, where we went on board. We first reached an Indian village, the only one I was fortunate enough to see in

America. Of course manners and customs have greatly changed with the natives since the days when their fathers, like our own, "hunted on their mountains, or fished in their rivers, their bodies painted in all the fantastic colours of barbarism." Still they are a primitive people, earning their livelihood by making, after the ancient pattern, mats, model canoes, and curiosities of various kinds. Their village contains a good many houses, all of a very humble character.

But there is one of which they are said to be very proud—their Court House—where they manage their political affairs; for it seems, this semi-savage race is trusted with something of Home Rule. Their pride, however, may be chiefly in the structure itself —apparently the only stone one they possess—more than in the self-government granted them. To prevent any danger of dismemberment, and to form a link of connection with the Empire, the Canadian Government supply each of the natives with a blanket once a year! And this is no doubt amply sufficient as a sure bond of union!

Much has been done for these Indians by the Christian community in efforts for their conversion and general elevation. The French were first in the field, and I believe a good many of the natives are Roman Catholics. Still, in this neighbourhood, and yet more fully elsewhere, a pure gospel has been preached to them, and with remarkable success. Some from the West have been trained for the ministry in the Colleges of New England, and have turned out faithful and eloquent pastors. But, strange enough, the great difficulty at first, when they go to school in civilized quarters, is to get them to go to bed. They prefer to wrap themselves in their blankets and lie on the floor.

It is said that all over Canada and the States, the Indians are by no means dying out, but keeping up their numbers wonderfully. And as a whole, they are content with their lot, and much pleased when employed by the white man to attend him in fishing, and in the chase. The limited territory, however, to which they are confined is keenly felt by many of their chiefs. I heard of one who was sitting on the grass, engaged in earnest conversation with a Government official whom he asked, from time to time, to sit a little further, and again at little further, till the dignitary came against a tree, when he said, "What do you mean? I can go no further." "That is it," was the reply, "just what you have been doing to my people!"

Shortly after leaving the Indian village, "the rapids were near," but "the daylight was not past," as the early morning sun had just shone out, scattering his beams on the broad but rushing waters. I may remark here, that an additional charm was lent to this voyage from the fact that the Canadian Boat Song, to which I have alluded, refers to this scene, and was written by Moore while he was sailing on this part of the St. Lawrence.

As we approached the rapids, hearing the rushing noise, and being gradually drawn into the current, we could well understand how they were long thought to be impassable. And this impression would no doubt be confirmed, when the English, proceeding to take Montreal, in 1760, lost, between the upper rapids and those of Lachine, some sixty boats and a row-galley, with artillery stores and ammunition, and about ninety men. But indications were often given that there were certain openings where vessels might make the venture. Logs of wood were seen to move down without touching the rocks. The Indians, also, when carried over by accident, or occasionally, it might be, by design, made the passage in their canoes with perfect safety. It was, therefore, resolved to commit large vessels to their guidance, which they managed with success; and ultimately they became the pilots of steam-boats making the regular run. It was said that the four men at the wheel, stationed in an elevated position within view of all, were Indians. Of this we had our doubts—at least there was nothing of the red about them, though a good deal of the bronze. They seemed, however, to feel their importance and responsibility, holding the wheel firmly, and looking earnestly before them, as we approached the foaming waters and were being swept down the current.

The descent was considerable, and we were rapidly driven close by great rocks, over which the river was rushing and plunging. There was no smooth water, and the only course we could pursue was among breakers, some of which struck our bow as if there had been a storm. Yet there was no sense of danger, as we knew that numerous vessels had long gone this way, and that accidents of any kind were of rare occurrence. It was simply exhilarating, like coming in first at a boat race, with the waters dashing from our sides. But to those looking at us from the shore it must have seemed alarming, if the pictures of it are at all a faithful representation.

For a few miles after we left this interesting and exciting scene, we sailed on comparatively still waters, and between flat, but richly wooded banks. Then we passed under the Victoria Tubular Bridge, without requiring to bend our funnel, as is needful when much smaller crafts approach the bridges on the Thames or the Clyde. From this position we had some idea both of the height and apparent strength of the noble structure, which spans the river in a stretch within a few yards of two miles, and is, in every way, well worthy the name it bears. We landed near the mouth of an excellent canal, by which our steam-boat, and vessels that reach the city by the same route as we did, can go upwards and join the river above the rapids, which would be otherwise impossible. Of course, vessels may go by the canal both ways, and thus altogether avoid the difficulty. The advantage in taking the rapids is mainly the much greater speed thus acquired in descending, as compared with passing through the locks of a canal, a saving, I suppose, of considerably more than an hour.

After this short run up the St. Lawrence, and a pleasant day in Montreal, I had a long sail down the river—for about 180 miles—to Quebec. I started by the evening steamboat, which is one of the finest of its kind I have seen, not even excepting those on the Hudson. The saloon runs from stem to stern, leaving only small openings at the extremities, provided with glass doors through which to view the scenery from within, and giving access to the portion of the deck that extends beyond, where a limited number of passengers may go on fine weather, and enjoy the fresh air. As these are night-boats, extensive deck accommodation is not needed. All around the saloon are State-rooms, with berths arranged in double tiers, the whole under one roof, thus making the entire space enclosed as lofty as it is, in other respects, most spacious. These rooms furnish sufficient sleeping accommodation for several hundred passengers, and each one has his own key, so that he can secure his property within, and exclude all intruders who might disturb his retirement or repose.

Before retiring to rest, I was anxious to see as much as possible of the course we were pursuing, and lingered on the little deck outside, looking wistfully on the dark waters and the dim outline of the rocky banks, till I found I had been locked out; and only by gazing through, and knocking at the glass door, I succeeded, with some difficulty, in attracting the attention of those near it to my awkward position, when the steward was ultimately called and took the outcast in.

I slept soundly in my little room, but, unfortunately too long, for the sun had got up before me, and was already gilding, with his golden beams, the tinted woods that crowned or clung to the sides of the bold precipitous rocks which rose so proudly from the banks of the river. Much was thus missed. But the time occupied by my toilet was improved by taking furtive glances through my little window, at the lovely scenes through which we were now gently gliding, and it was not long till I was on deck taking in the whole at a glance. I had already seen and admired the American forests in something of their autumn splendour, but, touched with the more advanced frosts of the northern Canadian shores, these far excelled:

> " On sunny slope and beechen swell,
> The shadowed light of 'morning' fell ;
> And, where the maple's leaf was brown,
> With soft and silent lapse came down
> The glory, that the wood receives,
> At 'sunrise,' in its brazen leaves."

The reflection of these "brazen leaves" lay on the waters "like apples of gold in baskets of silver."

We were just approaching Point Levi, immediately opposite Quebec, when I left my berth. And there was the City, of which I heard so much, resting on, and rising above, these lofty crags, which seemed to form an impregnable barrier against sweeping tide or icy blocks, and every foe. I had sought, from early youth, to realise the surroundings of the famous siege, had often heard the praises of the scene from those accustomed to sail to it from our port, and had sometimes gone on board their ships to welcome them home, and taste the waters of the St. Lawrence, drawn directly, pure and sweet, from that broad strong flood. These associations doubtless helped to encircle this rocky-brow with a certain halo. But it has a grandeur all its own. There is no city I know of that has a situation like it, except it may be Edinburgh. Yet it is not equal to Edinburgh in variety of striking natural objects, mingled with soft beauty; and in the possession of numerous graceful modern structures, relieved by lofty and ancient picturesque dwellings. Quebec is somewhat grim and gray, lacking in the grassy slopes and gardens which, from almost every point of view, give such a charm to the Scottish capital. Still, if it has less of the lovely, it has much of the bold and picturesque. It is built on a tongue of land, formed by the meeting of the waters of the St. Lawrence and the Charles rivers. At its base there is a narrow strip of flat rock, extending all around the peninsula, where the old town finds shelter immediately under the shadow of the great natural bulwarks which rise precipitously above. Here also are the docks, wharves, ferry-piers, and buildings connected with the commerce of the city.

When we landed I made at once for the upper city. There are three different means of ascent to this; either by a long winding carriage way, or by steep stairs forming a narrow street, or by an elevator. I preferred the last, though the least dignified, perhaps because I was getting accustomed to the mechanical habits of the Americans; or, as I reasoned with myself, because I had the prospect, in returning, of taking either of the other ways, so much more easy in the descent, and might thus husband my time and strength for the long day's work before me.

Fortified by an early breakfast on shore, I at once commenced my attack on the ramparts, citadel, and walls, that had frowned on us from below. First, from the battlements that are crowned by Durham and Dufferin Terraces, I looked down on the market, still crowded with busy buyers and sellers of supplies for the morning, whilst the river swept rapidly and unceasingly by their side. Then I gazed long from Cape Diamond—fully 330 feet above the waters directly under it—and wandered among the fortifications of the Citadel, with soldiers guarding, but with perfect liberty to pass. Here I overlooked not a narrow stream, but a mighty river, more than a mile broad at its narrowest part, and swelling out, at the meeting of the waters, to something like a large lake, several miles broad. The Island of Orleans, at a distance of about a dozen miles, bounds the view in front, and breaks the river into two branches. On the north bank the rocks rise precipitously, at the upper edge of which a long range of houses stretches for nearly eight miles from the falls of Montmorenci, which we faintly see like a silver chain lying over the crags. These houses are built chiefly of gray limestone, finely contrasting with the dark background; and in the midst of the line we detected a church with two lofty towers, and learned that it is that of which Father Chiniquy was the popular priest, whose conversion to Protestantism, and the zeal and success with which he maintained and extended gospel truth, together with the persecution to which he was, and still is exposed, have made his name familiar on both sides of the Atlantic. The mountains beyond these houses rise at first gradually, with signs of considerable cultivation, and then swell into lofty ridges, clothed with wood up to their summits. Point Levi is on the opposite side of the St. Lawrence, where the banks also are steep, and studded with numerous buildings, public and private, and with places around, which are favourite resorts with the inhabitants of Quebec for summer quarters.

Leaving the Citadel I was attracted by the massive Parliament Buildings—not yet completed, but in use—situated on a commanding position, with a magnificent prospect, overlooking the entire city, its forts, ramparts and all. I inspected the various halls and apartments, which are really very fine, and lingered a little in the gallery of the Chamber of Representatives, listening to the Speaker's daughter, unconscious of any audience, discoursing sweet music on a piano which had been left there from a reception on the previous day. I was surprised to learn that the debates here are conducted promiscuously in French and in English, and that fully three-fourths of the population of Quebec are French. I had afterwards manifest proof of this as I wandered through the city. Its proclamations and advertisements were generally in both languages; the children, hastening to school, were gabbling chiefly in the foreign tongue; and a cabman, whom I had occasion to hire, would give me excellent information in good English, with an Irish flavour, and then turn to the tollman and make a passing remark in fluent French.

My great object was to reach the Plains of Abraham, little more than a mile beyond the Parliament Buildings. The road is lined nearly all the way with neat, and sometimes handsome, residences. The Plains themselves, however, have remained unbroken, except it may be by horses' hoofs; for there is an old Stand on the ground, which indicates that it was for a while, if it is not still, used as a race-course. It was deeply interesting to walk on this broad plateau, on the edge of the cliffs, where Wolfe, after a long and weary siege, in 1759, gained the victory, which virtually secured for Britain the entire Continent of North America, and which, despite the separation of the States, is really the possession of the Anglo-Saxon race to this day. But it was solemn to stand on the spot where the great hero bled and died; and where, at the moment of victory, he uttered the remarkable words, so unlike the language of war, "God be praised, I die in peace;" having shortly before repeated Gray's Elegy, with special emphasis on the line, soon to be so appropriate in his own case, "The path of glory leads but to the grave." A pillar, crowned with a helmet and sword, marks the fatal spot.

I returned to Quebec by St. John's Gate, which is a little more than a mile from the Plains. Close beside it, Montcalm, the general who led the French forces against Wolfe, fell, and died before the dawn of the following day. Thus the same battle-field was alike fatal to the victorious and vanquished commanders.

I walked round the city walls, which are clearly marked and strong. Though no longer available in these days as a protection, they are interesting in themselves, and for the scenes they open up. I passed through the principal streets, which are always varied, sometimes curious, and marked by good public buildings, with numerous churches and other ecclesiastical edifices. I also lingered at the Grand Battery and Esplanade, viewing the city, the meeting of the waters, and the mountains beyond dotted with scattered villages. I found there was still time for a drive in the neighbourhood, which I was glad to take, partly as a rest after the long day's toil on foot, and as furnishing an opportunity of seeing something more which it would have been a pity to have missed.

My cabman took me by the suburbs that overlook the Charles River on to St. Foye, where a monument marks the scene of a victory gained by the French, after the defeat under Wolfe, but which had very temporary results. Then we drove across the country to the St. Lawrence, by an earth road, till we reached the top of a deep ravine, which it was thought no one could scale, till the Highlanders, on their way to the Plains of Abraham, climbed it like monkeys, and showed that there was a path here both to battle and to victory. Another, though a more peaceful and prosaic proof that these rocks can be scaled, has since then been given in the construction of a zig-zag road, down which my driver proceeded, where horse and cab made many and varied angles with each other, and went twisting and screwing, and, in spite of the screeching brake, threatened, at every corner, to plunge us over some yawning precipice. By this means we reached Wolfe's Cove, which bears the name of the General, as being the place where he landed to attack Quebec—having previously led his men across the river, through the darkness, all in profound silence, and in boats with muffled oars.

From Wolfe's Cove, where the old town begins, we drove along its single street—for there is no space for more than one between the river on the one hand, and the precipitous rocks on the other. The houses are chiefly built of wood, and must have lasted for many generations, and, to all appearance, might well have been occupied by the original colonists. Some of them are oddly perched on craggy corners, not always facing the street, but looking in various directions, often seeming to defy the law of gravitation, and in such a dilapidated condition as would delight the heart of an artist to behold. The northern nations of Europe here compete with the French in the struggle for existence; their presence being manifest in the rough unpronounceable names by which they advertise themselves, and in an antique Scandinavian Church, whose quaint wooden architecture and inscription proclaimed its nationality.

We rose to the new town by a steep winding carriage way, lined with houses and shops which it must have cost a good deal of engineering skill to put into position. After dinner I purposed walking down by the street formed of continuous steps, up which I had looked in the morning and admired its picturesque appearance, when I preferred the elevator. I thought I would have ample time to do this, and catch the boat that crossed to Point Levi in connection with the train that was to take me back to Montreal. I found, however, that I had miscalculated the distance, and as it was doubtful if I would gain my purpose, I was compelled to take my cabman again, whom I had dismissed, but who, knowing my circumstances, was carefully waiting his opportunity. He soon drove me, with Jehu-like speed, down the steep cork-screw street we had previously, with difficulty, struggled up; so that, at every turn, I expected horse and all would suddenly appear in the heart of some china or jeweller's shop, with what results we might faintly imagine.

I was just in time for the steam-ferry, on board of which, and for a while on the other side of the river, I had a conversation with a gentleman connected with the Quebec Press, when I felt more anxious to be the interviewer than the interviewed. He gave me rather a dark account of the condition and prospects of the city and neighbourhood. This I had afterwards confirmed, and given more in detail, by others well-informed on the subject. I learned that the people were rapidly growing poorer, and that the province was going backward, not only because the trade was partially leaving it, but for want of proper cultivation, and on account of the pernicious power granted to the Roman Catholics. Farmers are heavily taxed by the priests in order to build enormous churches and cathedrals; also to erect and maintain needless sectarian hospitals and colleges, with numerous nunneries and monasteries. None of these institutions bear any of the burdens for the general support of the country, while all ecclesiastics are equally exempted. And, strange to say, though the State has thus no power to tax church property, or the priests, for the common good, it has given the priests power to enforce tithes from their people for sectarian ends. This legal authority furnishes them with an additional weapon for oppression, and gives them the strongest motive to buy up all farms belonging to Protestants — whom they cannot tax for strictly religious purposes. They are accordingly making extensive purchases of land, which they sometimes retain and cultivate themselves, or sell to their own people at an interest of four per cent. on the capital invested; for which fourteen per cent. in all is thus paid.

Is it not truly astonishing that, after the connection between Church and State has nominally ceased in Canada, we are still, through a large portion of the Dominion, leaving the powers of the State in the hands of the Roman Catholic Hierarchy to such an extent as to enable them by force to support their religion, thus oppressing their people, widening more and more the gulf which separates the two races, and draining the British population gradually from the soil! My friend of the Press declared that a revolution was imminent. This may be an extreme view; but I find, from several Canadian newspapers, that, at public meetings, both in this Province and beyond it, strong expressions are being employed regarding this condition of affairs. One of the clergymen of Toronto, whose fellowship I have enjoyed since I was there, and several gentlemen with whom I conversed when I was in Canada, all alike declare that there is something radically wrong, which the prosperity and safety of the Province urgently requires should be rectified.

No doubt the French Canadians are loyal to British rule, loving our Government and laws as apparently they do not those now prevailing in the land of their fathers. They are also, as a whole, a peaceful and contented people, with much that is amiable and excellent in their character, and having men of intelligence and public spirit among them. But their contentment is carried so far as to be one of their great weaknesses; for they have little of the push and desire to make progress, useful everywhere, but most essential in a new country. They are generally satisfied to remain in the same farm, and cultivate it after the same manner, as their fathers did. And they seem generally to approve and defend the special powers, and so-called privileges, of their church; though they can scarcely fail to see that these are not proving a blessing, but bringing a blight on the very soil. Some, however, both see and express this, and have taken the spoiling of their goods rather than submit. We heard of more than one farmer, during our visit, who had made a stand, and whose produce was likely to be sold to meet the demand of the priests.

It must be acknowledged that there are many serious obstacles in the way of reform. The present powers in the hands of the priesthood were granted by treaty between France and Britain when Canada was conquered. All parties in the contract might thus require to be consulted, and much opposition would doubtless be raised. But why should it be impossible to rescind a treaty, entered into nearly a hundred and thirty years ago, now that it is found to operate most unjustly and injuriously on the general community? The possession of a separate Parliament by Quebec, with full powers to manage local affairs in connection with the general Government at Ottawa, which is enjoyed by all the other provinces in the Dominion, is not the difficulty. No one seeks to deprive them of this, and all the Canadians seem thoroughly satisfied with the system of federation. Every one of the States in the American Union has also a Parliament of its own, invested with large local powers, but none of them is permitted to make enactments of any kind that would interfere with complete religious equality. And why should not the authority given to the Canadian Provinces be the same, and in every one of them alike, State powers being employed only for State purposes, and a fair field and no favour given to all religions? This is the only way of solving the difficulty, and it is the only way of avoiding a similar difficulty should federation be granted nearer home. Exempting Protestant ministers from national taxation, so as to put them, in this respect, on a level with the priests, is preventing them from discharging a patriotic duty, and is only a sop by which they may be induced to utter a feeble protest against, and a means of confirming and extending, existing evils. Where this has been offered it should be refused, and where it has been accepted it should be relinquished, that, with free and clean hands, it may be insisted that the rule be applied all round. No remnants of that power which has wrought, and is still working, such mischief, should be allowed to remain.

But we have wandered from the line of our travels. However important these questions may be, we must not be carried too far aside by them. Let us, therefore, hasten to the end of this part of our story.

After crossing the St. Lawrence, from Quebec to Point Levi, I proceeded by train, on the south side of the river, toward Montreal. For fully a hundred miles the country continued extremely uninteresting, except as a picture of solitude and desolation. The whole was over-run with brushwood; the trees, in some districts, lifting up their bare blackened stems and diminished branches, the result apparently of forest fires. A few lonely log houses, and insignificant villages with little or no signs of life and activity around them, were passed at considerable intervals. And yet, I understand that at one time this was largely a grain producing district, but, under exhaustive mismanagement, has returned to its wilderness condition, requiring centuries either for the primeval forest to grow, or the virgin soil to be re-formed.

Shortly before darkness set in there were signs of improvement. We crossed some lovely streams, and called at a few towns, where water and steam-power were used to carry on wood-cutting and other businesses. Hence, as we swept along in the dark, I was enabled to picture to myself what was hidden as in a more hopeful condition than what I had seen. But the sight of our Canadian Cottage, when the evening was far advanced, was a pleasing reality which brought refreshment and rest, specially welcome to limbs weary with delightful toil.

CHAPTER X.

To Boston.

WE had the privilege of a Sabbath in Canada to refresh both body and spirit before returning to the United States. In the forenoon we worshipped in Ersskine Church, Montreal, pleased to find that the good Seceders have a name and a place here. This is one of the largest and most beautiful Presbyterian Churches in the city. But others, such as Knox Church, St. Paul's, and St. Andrew's—which I could only survey from the outside—are not behind it in appearance. and they all stand somewhat on a par in the influence for good which they exercise throughout the Dominion and in distant parts.

Among the Presbyterians generally, who have about a dozen congregations in Montreal, and among the other Protestant denominations in Canada, there is a close and kindly fellowship; for, though the names that indicate the old landmarks in the progress of Christian liberty at home may sometimes be retained, one, at least, of the separating influences has disappeared. All are in the same relation to the State; and, with the exception of the congregation of St. Andrew's, the Presbyterians have formed an incorporate union, by which they are enabled to maintain ordinances, and their various colleges and other religious enterprises, to an extent, and with an economy, that would otherwise have been impossible.

The Roman Catholics of Montreal, who are chiefly composed of the original French inhabitants and immigrants of that persuasion who have come out since, number fully half of the population. The most magnificent churches in the city are certainly theirs. That of Notre-Dame has long been famous, and stands out as a prominent feature in the landscape. Its interior, which we visited during the week, is equal in many respects to some of the most celebrated churches in France or Italy. But a yet greater has been growing up, and is now approaching completion, in the most fashionable quarter. This is St. Peter's, the great dome of which rises to a height of about 250 feet, and the whole is constructed after the model of its name-sake in Rome. As the result of these special efforts in the cause, it is said that the priests in Montreal cherish the expectation that they may, ere long, be able to induce the Pope to cast in his lot as an immigrant among them, so that he may escape the imprisonment which, he says, he is enduring in his own capital. Would it not be interesting if this should be realised, and the head of the Church be tempted to desert his historical home, so that the building of this vast structure might have an issue not unlike that which was brought about by the erection of the Roman original, which was an important factor in promoting the Reformation?

On Sabbath evening I worshipped in Longueuil. Here are only a Roman Catholic and an Episcopalian Church. The Episcopalian is attended by the English-speaking population of all denominations; Presbyterians and congregationalists alike taking part in the choir, and otherwise assisting in its services. The preaching and worship are somewhat in harmony with these circumstances, and have nothing of the high tendencies sometimes found in the old country. They see too much of the full development of Ritualism in the midst of them to make them desirous to copy it. The Roman Catholics in this town are building what may be called a Cathedral, whose roof and towers already, with imposing elevation, overlook the city of Montreal and a large stretch of the St. Lawrence. We inspected the progress of the work within, and found that though roof and walls were finished, the great pillars and arches were only being formed. Each pillar consisted of a rough beam, with a large circle of wicker-work around, lathed and receiving a few coats of plaster, so as to make the whole seem a mass of solid marble. Is not this somewhat typical?

Early in the week, and early in the morning, we left Canada by a totally different route from that by which we had approached it. Our previous journey had been varied by roaring cataracts, broad lakes, and a mighty river. This took us far inland by comparatively quiet scenes. But it was not without its interest. There was a certain charm in plunging at once into the heart of a forest where we saw many "lifting up the axe upon the thick trees." Log huts frequently appeared, not neglected and sad like those opposite Quebec, but with every sign of joyous activity around them. In their natural situation they were picturesque, and brought up something of my ideal of primitive Canadian life. Stories, pictures, and dreams of the backwoods were vividly recalled, and I felt as if I were now in the midst of all these fancies realised in facts. Was it not, therefore, provoking soon to discover that I had been investing with this halo of romance, not pioneers making clearances for new homes, but navvies making a new railway! Yet why should we despise their honest toil? Are not such men doing a noble work, bringing a reward to those who felled "the forest primeval," and making a way which at once marks the path of past, and opens up the prospect of future progress?

It was not long till we were out of the wood. Canada was left behind, and we were once more in the United States. Here we had a charming welcome in the opening up immediately of Lake Champlain with its sparkling waters and bold lovely banks. This is one of the *small* lakes of America, being only five times the length of our longest, or 126 miles. We drove along from its lower to its upper extremity, keeping generally very close to its west shore, and never losing sight of the *green* mountains of Vermont (does the State derive its name from these?) on the opposite shore. In thus being able to see across the lake, Champlain has a picturesque character which none of the vast inland fresh water seas, between Canada and the States, possesses. Though we could not view it at once in its length, we could easily do so in its breadth, which never exceeds twelve miles; and there are often opposite capes within a mile of each other, while towards its head, it continues for a considerable distance no broader than a river. It is said to have about fifty islands; and these, with the innumerable creeks and bays that break the shore, and the lofty crags that overlook it, casting their deep shadows on the water, present an endless and pleasing variety. Sometimes we suddenly turn round a rocky corner on the brink of a precipice, when, far as the eye can reach, the islands are seen like emeralds on the silver sheen; at other times we sweep round a pebbly beach, or dip into the land, to find cultivated fields and farm houses, not unlike our own. At many points, Lake Champlain reminded me of Loch Lomond, only the width here is generally greater, and the view consequently less striking. And there is no Ben Lomond rising head and shoulders above all.

Before we reach the head of the lake the railway goes some distance into it, where we find a station erected on piles, forming a broad platform, with all the requisite buildings—ticket office, waiting rooms, &c., attached—and a Pier; the whole resembling an ancient lake-dwelling restored. Here a steamboat calls, when there is an exchange of passengers, requiring a longer stoppage than usual. We step out for a few minutes, and are immediately recognised by a lady, and then by her husband, who, with their son, came over with us in the *Republic*, and were travelling through the States. It is remarkable what friendship gushes forth at such unexpected and unlikely meetings on the part of those who, a few weeks before, were total strangers. We discovered that we were all purposing to return at the same time by the *Brittanic*; which we did, greatly enjoying and valuing their society.

It was a disappointment, shortly afterwards, to pass within sight of Lake George and not be permitted to visit it. In asking tickets for it at Montreal, we learned that the navigation had just been closed for the season; not as yet by ice, but by the stoppage of the usual communication. This was all the more trying, as the mountain pass, which we saw open into it, was evidently a gateway into grandeur and beauty of no ordinary kind. The scenery all around was of the true Highland type, and we doubt not but that Lake George, had we seen it, would have turned out a little gem worthy of all the praises of its warm admirers.

We were only about an hour in the famous city of Saratoga—the great Sanitorium of America. We could therefore do little more than look along its principal streets, lined with lofty elms, and survey its enormous hotels, one of which is said to have a thousand rooms, and accommodation for two thousand guests. There was no time either to taste of its healing springs or visit its lake.

In the afternoon, Albany was reached, which we had left about a week before on our way north; the circuit thus completed being thirteen hundred miles. The remainder of the day was spent in this, the capital of the State of New York. Climbing a steep ascent from the Railway Station, we soon found ourselves in a Square, small but imposing, formed chiefly by large public buildings. A gentleman whom we asked to identify these to us, responded most cordially, and then took us through the Capitol. This of course is the great lion of Albany, and it is said there is nothing superior to it except the Capitol of Washington. It is larger than that of Philadelphia, but not so lofty. It is not yet completed, though it was commenced sixteen years ago, in 1871, and has already cost twenty million dollars. In external architecture it is massive and dignified, while its porches, passages, halls, and innumerable apartments, most of them finished and in use, are on a most extensive scale, and fitted up with truly palatial splendour. What a rage there is at present, both in the old and the new world, for these huge State and Municipal buildings! Almost every great city is erecting one, and each striving to excel. Bulk, as well as beauty and usefulness, appear to be the general aim. Is not the spirit thus manifested much the same as that which led to the raising of the Tower of Babel, the Pyramids of Egypt, or the Cathedrals of Europe in the medieval times?

Our generous guide through the Capitol, willing to suggest to us other sights, asked how much time we had to spare. About three hours, I replied. "Three hours for Albany!" he said, "too bad, too bad!" He was evidently a citizen of some importance, as we gathered from his influence and whole bearing, and felt the insult all the more on that account. But the feeling is the same with all classes everywhere. Each citizen identifies his own honour with that of the town and State to which he belongs, and hence the rivalry which, if it sometimes leads to a desire to make things colossal rather than useful, is yet a powerful stimulus to progress, and, in the main, most healthy. It is certainly better far than a centralisation which enfeebles the extremities by depriving them of wholesome independent action.

We took a car and drove to the Park, passing through the most interesting parts of the city. As we returned, the electric lights were shedding their silver beams, imprinting, in strong shadow, on green sward and beaten highway, the branches and individual leaves of the fine trees that lined our entire course. In the Square, to which we returned, we noticed a splendid equipage, such as we seldom saw in America, consisting of a carriage and four, and learned that it was waiting for the Roman Catholic Archbishop, whom we afterwards met driving through the city, with a train of priests in humbler conveyances, followed by a small crowd of curious spectators. Surely this kingdom cometh not without observation— all needed to keep up appearances in this free Republic.

The loud noise of steam, evidently escaping from the funnel of a vessel, attracted us to the harbour. Wandering along the quay we observed a railway bridge, and were tempted to cross the Hudson by a footpath which we discovered ran inside the parapet. At this point—about a hundred-and-fifty miles from the sea—the navigation of steamboats and large vessels ceases, and these were seen lying close at hand, safely moored for the night. Above the bridge there is communication for smaller craft, both by the river and by means of two great canals; the one, nearly two hundred miles long, coming from Lake Erie, and the other, much shorter, coming from Lake

Champlain, and connected with Lake Ontario. We stood for some time on the bridge endeavouring to trace the signs of commercial activity in the numerous masts that dimly appeared in the darkness, and admiring the various lamps whose broken reflections were scattered on the dark rolling river. Lights, also, on barges and rafts, carried down by the current, silently and mysteriously glided under us like water-kelpies; while every now and again a glaring engine, with glowing carriages behind, would dash and roar just at our side, on the trembling bridge, whose wooden way acted as a too sensitive sounding board.

The evening was somewhat advanced when we left for Boston. This was the most uncomfortable ride, we may say the only uncomfortable ride, we had during all our western tour. First, an attempt was made to light our stove, but it was either new or untried for the season, and would not work, filling our carriage with smoke, which the perseverance of the guard to kindle a fire only continued to increase, to our great discomfort, till the attempt was given up in despair. Then, at the chilliest hour of the night, when we were about half way on our journey, all the passengers were turned out at Springfield station, where we had to remain, sleepy and without any means of rest, for three hours. Why this was we could not tell; but it might have been worse, as we perceive from the American newspapers, that, on this same line and near this same spot, an accident occurred shortly afterwards, when three cars took fire and were burned, one passenger being burned to death, and nineteen injured.

It was early in the morning when we approached Boston, and a slight hoar-frost lay on the ground, giving the prospect of a cool day, always welcome when a good deal of walking had to be done. Landing in the heart of the city, and refreshed by a hearty breakfast, at which I could suppose nearly a hundred sat down, we were ready for a day's exploration. We strolled through several streets, with their splendid shops and warehouses, and looked at a few of the more interesting buildings, such as the oldest church, and Faneuil Hall—the "cradle of liberty," where many excited gatherings were held in the stirring times. Some of the streets, with all their modern business aspect, have a certain old-world character about them, not being formed on the rectangular principle, which prevails elsewhere in the States, but often narrow, bending and turning from each other at every possible angle. No wonder that this should be the case when we remember that Boston was founded by the Pilgrim Fathers, not more than ten years after their landing at Plymouth Rock, and that they planned these streets apparently from the home pattern. This was interesting; but it had its drawback, for we felt that in spite of an excellent map, we might easily wander amid these intricacies, and time was too precious for that experience.

So we leapt on a car with "Bunker's Hill" marked upon it, as that spot was one of our great attractions to Boston. This famous historical height rises in the midst of Charlestown, a suburb which we reached by one of the numerous ways, formed by dykes with drawbridges in the centre, crossing the Charles River. The monument erected on the summit is a granite obelisk, 221 feet high, fully double the height of Nelson's monument in Edinburgh. There is a winding stair within, by which to ascend to the top, but no elevator's aid—probably felt to be out of place where so much hardness had been endured—and we have to go step by step to gain the lofty pinnacle. But who would grudge the climb when such a scene is suddenly revealed? Beneath and before us is the City, with its watery surroundings breaking it into capes, and peninsulas, and islands; and forming bays, and creeks, and channels, and docks, and a mystic river; all in immediate connection with the ocean, and embracing a scene of life and beauty at once marvellous and picturesque. It is said that there are upwards of forty islands, great and small, within this spacious but strangely tortuous harbour; one of the largest and safest from storms, and best protected against an enemy, to be found anywhere.

With our "view of Boston from Bunker's Hill" we endeavoured to distinguish the chief places of interest in sight. But the revelations of the past, and identifying these with the scenes before us, constituted the great attraction. There is the part of the harbour where lay the ships with their cargoes of tea—taxed without the consent of the country—which fifty daring men boarded, breaking up the contents and scattering them on the water in the silence of the night, when multitudes, with breathless interest, heard only the sound of the axes and hammers. This was the first act of rebellion against the British Government (or rather against a foolish king and his foolish counsellors), and known afterwards as "The Boston teaparty." Shortly afterwards, on the hill where we stood, the first battle of the great Revolution was fought, amid the burning of the dwellings around; while the dreadful scene was beheld by thousands of spectators who crowded the roofs and steeple-towers of the city on the opposite side of the water; and where, after a brief but terrible struggle, five hundred Americans, and eleven hundred English soldiers, lay dead, literally saturating with their blood this small summit and these grassy slopes. The victory in the end was on the side of the British forces, and therefore we thought it strange that the Americans should raise such a noble monument on this spot. But the moral victory was certainly with the Americans, showing what even their undisciplined arms could do, and rousing the whole country to the aid of Boston; so that here "freedom's battle was begun," which, though much bitterness and awful destruction followed, has, under the control of "Him who makes the wrath of man to praise Him," greatly advanced the cause of civil and religious liberty throughout the world. Little carved stones are fixed all round the hill, marking carefully the places where officers commanded, and companies stood to the fight, or fell.

We spent some time on Boston Common, inferior in size and ornament to most of the American Parks; but superior to all of them in national interest. It was formed shortly after the city was founded; and an ancient tree, which existed in the days of the Pilgrim Fathers, stood here till about ten years ago, called "the tree of liberty," whose broken stem we found still guarded by iron rails. On this Common, British and American soldiers often assembled and exercised, not for parade, but in the midst of scenes of actual warfare. It was interesting for us to see a military encampment here, and wait and witness a review on its gently sloping sward. The beautiful public gardens closely connected with it, and separated only by a street unbuilt upon, and the handsome public buildings and private residences appearing through the trees in every other direction, give an aspect of wealth and taste to the entire neighbourhood. We climbed to the top of the State House, which is situated at one end of the Common, and commands a fine view of the city. To this position we were raised by means of an elevator, the use of which, with permission to visit every part of the premises, is free; because, as we were told, it is the property of the people—a frequent experience and assurance given to visitors of public buildings in America.

From this we took a car to the interesting suburb of Cambridge, passing to it over the water by a causeway, fully half a mile in length, which reminded one of reaching Venice by rail. There is an air of quiet dignity and learned leisure about the town, which surrounds the numerous college buildings. The colleges themselves are arranged without much regard to formal order, on a large green park, interspersed with noble trees. As a whole, Cambridge is not unworthy to bear the name of the great seat of learning in England, and has even in some respects a resemblance to it, with less of the mathematical in its structure, as it has less of the mathematical in its culture. Its existence is due to the Pilgrim Fathers, who established it six years after they began to build Boston, and its 250th anniversary has just been celebrated.

About seven years ago there was a much more imposing ceremony in commemoration of the foundation of the city of Boston, which dates from September 1630. Numerous deputies were present, as well as a vast concourse of the general public, from all parts of the United States; military reviews were got up—Mr. Beecher appearing conspicuous at the head of one of the regiments; great meetings were held for the delivery of patriotic addresses; and there was a special novelty in the form of tableaux, consisting of groups of citizens dressed after the manner of the times and characters represented, and arranged so as to give something like a living realisation of such scenes as the landing of the Norsemen, the landing of the Pilgrim Fathers at Plymouth Rock, Samuel Adams demanding the removal of the British Troops, the throwing of the tea overboard, Washington entering Boston, &c., &c. There were sixteen of these tableaux in all, the gentlemen forming them being raised on railway horse-cars, or lorries, driven through the crowded streets at night, and shown to full advantage by a brilliant torch-light procession. A friend from Scotland, who was present, told me it was not only a most striking but a most interesting and instructive occasion; and a handsome volume which I have seen, with a full account of the whole, and fine engravings of the tableaux, fully corroborates this.

The University at Cambridge, founded by and called after Harvard, is both the oldest and wealthiest in America. It has chairs for all the branches of learning commonly taught in the universities of the old country, and it is not behind many of these in the number and attainments of its professors and students. From a published report, which I obtained in the town, I find that it has at present 178 instructors, 29 other officers, and 1595 students. The College buildings are fifteen in number, and the grounds include fifteen acres.

Our survey of the University was chiefly external, and our thoughts were more of those who had passed away, than of those who still teach within its walls. The figure of Longfellow, more than that of any other, seemed to haunt the place, every corner of which must have been most familiar to him, as for some fifty years he trod these grassy lawns and shady streets, and during most of that period taught in one of these classrooms. Here we look on the slow-flowing Charles, which the poet so tenderly loved, and of which he thus sings :—

> "River that in silence windest
>   Through the meadows bright and free,
> Till at length thy rest thou findest
>   In the bosom of the sea!
>
> Four long years of mingled feeling,
>   Half in rest and half in strife,
> I have seen thy waters stealing
>   Onward, like the stream of life."

We crossed the river at a point referred to in the well-known song, familiar at every hearth where sweet music and natural English poetry are cherished :—

> "I stood on the bridge at midnight,
>   As the clocks were striking the hour,
> And the moon rose o'er the city,
>   Behind the dark church tower."

As not more than a mile distant were the waters of the ocean, whose " sea-weed floated wide," we could understand all the better, many allusions in the poem, and specially appreciate such a verse as this :—

> "Yet whenever I cross the river,
>   On its bridge with wooden piers,
> Like the odour of brine from the ocean
>   Comes the thought of other years."

It was at Cambridge, among the scenes which he thus so tenderly celebrates, that Longfellow passed away, only some five years ago. Next to him we can realise Lowell, who also makes the same neighbourhood classical through several of his pieces, not least through his "Indian-Summer Reverie," and who was born at Boston, and succeeded Longfellow in the chair of Modern Languages and Literature. Then we have Emerson, whose mystic dreamings many an admiring audience endeavoured vainly to comprehend, while he never failed to gather them together within some of these walls. And we have the venerable poet Whittier—now in his eightieth year—still residing in his native district, not far off. All these, with the exception, possibly, of the last, were members of the "Saturday Club," where much genial criticism and mutual stimulus must have been given, of which, unfortunately, we have no record. Long before any of these notables, Boston and its neighbourhood were familiar to Benjamin Franklin, as he first saw the light here, and here learned that fluency of speech, and that happy use of the pen and the type, which made his influence so powerful in the

Councils of his nation, and brought him to stand before kings. Well might all this give a charm to our visit to the celebrated New England City, and its sister University. Nor can we wonder that the memory of this galaxy of men of genius, and the spirit that still prevails here, have led the Bostonians to claim that theirs is the centre of learning in America. It is said that the boast in New York is, what a man *has*; in Philadelphia, what he *is*; and in Boston, what he *knows*.

We lingered amongst these surroundings and associations till the day was far advanced, when we set out for New York by the coast line, regretting that we could not turn aside to see Plymouth Rock, and that we had only the pale rays of the moon to enable us to look " on the wild new England shore." By means of this friendly light, however, we often saw the glittering seas shine between the rocks and bays; and we had also the assistance of the most brilliant artificial lights to reveal, for a little, such cities as Hartford and New Haven, where we made brief stoppages—though we were unable withal to find in the latter any trace of her famous Yale College.

The quantity of brush-wood and wilderness land which we passed through for considerable distances, both on approaching and on leaving Boston, greatly surprised us. Surely the ground must have been under better cultivation in the days of the hardy

Pilgrim Fathers. Has it been exhausted by their successors, who have sought rather to cultivate learning and luxurious habits? Or has the rush to the virgin soil of the West led to the abandonment of the more stubborn soil of the East? We cannot tell, but in any case it is a pity that what nursed the true nobility of the Republic should be thus neglected.

We reached New York when the great city was retiring to rest, but while its streets were still ablaze with electric lights. We had been absent from it only some eleven days, and yet what varied, delightful, and instructive experiences we had passed through during a journey of about 1,900 miles! We received a most cordial welcome in what we had begun to call our home there, and found, in renewed fellowship with friends, a "rest and be thankful," grateful for past enjoyment, and hopeful and refreshed for what might still be in store for us.

CHAPTER XI.

Across the Alleghanies.

EFORE leaving Scotland I learned that there was the prospect of a trip to the North Western States in the company of a few friends. I had no idea from this, however, of the great treat that was before me, and that, toward its close, I was to have the most interesting feature of my American tour.

A gentleman, connected with Broadway Tabernacle, had arranged to take his friend and pastor, Dr. Taylor, on this journey, in his private car, and I was to accompany them. Our generous host was H. B. Hammond, Esq., who has charge of the " Indiana, Decatur, and Springfield Railroad," which passes through a portion of Illinois and Indiana—about the centre of the Continent—and which he had occasion to visit about this time. We were glad to find that Mr. Hammond could also take with him his brother-in-law, Mr. Bates, a young gentleman connected with the legal profession. This was the circle, or rather the quartette, varied yet harmonious, which set out to enjoy each other, and wide and novel scenes, for at least ten days.

The mode of travelling by private car was altogether new to me, and I may be excused for attempting to describe it somewhat minutely. When proceeding by lines belonging to other companies, which we had most frequently occasion to do, a position at the end of the train furthest from the engine was always secured for us. Our parlour was at the extremity of our car, with glass windows occupying the entire space on three sides, so that we had the most complete command of the scenes opening up to the right and left, and those spreading out far behind. Here we could recline on sofas, sit on fixed easy chairs, or shift an ordinary chair according to convenience, generally gazing one way while we were going in another. It was altogether peculiar to look at the rails, ever pouring out from beneath us like cables spinning from a rope-work, rapidly receding and coming closer and closer in perspective, till at last they appeared as if blended into one.

Next to the parlour was the drawing-room, with couches on either side, where we might retire at any time for a little solitude, or to have a quiet talk with one of the friends. This was fitted up in the evening as a bed-room, with four berths, two on either side, each curtained off from the other. A special luxury from the arrangement of the berths was that we could remain each under his blankets after the morning dawned, and, without turning the head, look out on the ever-changing landscape sweeping past. If we did not fall asleep at once in the darkness, which we generally did, or awake before the day, which we seldom did, we might study the silent stars and the silver moon, so fixed and calm above the horizon, when all was fleeting and restless below—fit emblem of the contrast between earthly and heavenly things.

From the drawing-room there was a narrow passage close to the right side of the car, by which we could proceed to the dining-room, where, besides enjoying other luxuries, we could look on the view opening up before us, interrupted only by the nearest public car to which we were coupled. Between these two rooms on the left side of the passage was, first, the pantry, stored or regularly supplied with all needfuls—flesh, fowls, and fruit, with every variety of safe dainties; next, the kitchen, where dishes were cooked, tempting every palate that yet required no tempting; and then Mr. Hammond's private room, with writing desk and other conveniences for carrying on business. This last was, of course, specially useful when our motion ceased; but it was marvellous how practice had enabled Mr. Hammond to manipulate accounts, and carry on ordinary correspondence, with a pretty steady hand, even when we were rolling along at full speed. I wrote an epistle or so here, but unaccustomed as I am to the use of the pen in such circumstances, I must only have given perplexity and pain to my friends at home if they attempted to make out my meaning. Is it proper to say that I used a sharper instrument every morning to maintain a smooth countenance, and, though much caution was needed, I never thereby inflicted pain on myself?

I must not omit to notice here one of the most valuable and essential requisites to the completeness of our travelling comforts. This was our excellent coloured cook, Mr. Johnson, who attended to our every want, and prepared for the table in a way that was his pride, and our grateful boast. Mr. Johnson was a man of superior intelligence, at the head of a provident society of coloured people numbering about two thousand members. He told us that there were many such societies throughout the States, with a larger membership than his, founded on principles which I need not explain, but which seemed at once safe and economical.

It will thus be seen we had within ourselves all that heart could desire; that we were in fact a moving household with every home comfort. And as an Englishman's house is his castle, so is an American's car. None dare intrude without the consent of the owner; not even a guard disturbed us asking to inspect or to check tickets, for we needed none, and though he might look in occasionally to see that signal cords, &c., were right, it was seldom, and always with a gentlemanly apology. He might come to the little platform outside, at any time, to give signals by day, or arrange our lamps by night; and we might step out there too if we wished to speak with him, or to enjoy the strong fresh breeze that our motion never failed to create. The platform was protected by an iron rail, and a small gate was provided, by which we might leave the car at any station. But care was needed if we ventured into the open when the train was in full speed, lest a pin might have got loose by the shaking, and we should lean on the unfastened gate, be projected out, and left behind more than lamenting.

The ride from Jersey City to Philadelphia I had already taken, and have endeavoured to describe. I may only say here that, with new and special advantages to view them, the banks of the Delaware seemed more lovely, and the city of Penn, as we approached it, more attractive than before. A good deal of shunting was required to get us into position, but here, as everywhere during our journey, this was successfully accomplished, though not without much watchfulness and care on the part of our host; and soon we were passing rapidly through new and ever changing and charming scenes.

The country west of Philadelphia was more thoroughly under cultivation than any other portion of

America I had seen. For miles, on either side, there were fine residences and villas, separately or in groups, belonging chiefly to Philadelphian merchants, many of whom travel daily into the city. Beyond this we passed what are known as the Dutch model farms. The homes are small, made of neatly carved wood; the outhouses are out of all proportion, being lofty and spacious buildings of the same material, sharply cut in every corner, but plain and far from picturesque. All these farms turned up of exactly the same pattern, the walls painted in purest white, apparently in oil, with the window frames of strong red, bordered with blue. The fields are large but painfully uniform, each a perfect square or rectangle, surrounded by wooden pailings painted brilliantly in white, and the gates in red. It seemed as if the whole was rather for show than for use, standing out with striking effect on the fields and sloping ground behind, but with a formality which the Dutch alone can appreciate.

As we enter the Chester valley, beautiful natural scenery opens up, enlivened by farm houses of every form, and in every variety of situation. We pass some pleasing villages, and call at several thriving towns and cities, such as Downington, Lancaster, and Middletown. But it is not till we reach Harrisburg, the capital of Pennsylvania, that the grandeur of the scene begins to be disclosed. There is only a brief call made at this city, no more than sufficient to enable us to discover a few of its public works and excellent public buildings, and admire its fine situation, with two or three unusually extensive mansions in the neighbourhoods, such as Lochiel House and Kirkwood House.

The Susquehanna flows past Harrisburg, and is here about a mile broad, somewhat shallow, dotted over, and broken into endless basins and rivulets, by innumerable rocks and islands; while here and there, on the banks, we find neat cottages shaded in sequestered spots among the trees. A few miles above the city we cross the river by a bridge, from which, on account of its length—nearly 4,000 feet— and with the advantage of our crystal parlour, we are enabled, for a considerable distance, to take a full survey, both up and down, admiring the strangely speckled stream, and catching a glimpse of the lofty mountains, with the deep valley, where the river is lost in the distance.

We turn aside and follow the course of the Juniata, wending our way close beside that lovely stream as it glides or rushes between the mountains. We enter various narrows and creeks, which, at times, seem entirely to block up our way. In some places we were strikingly reminded of Killiecrankie, and at others there are openings with vales which look not unlike Newark on the Yarrow—the ruined castle of course being wanting. The deer and the roe find a home here, and one is sometimes seen standing on the line and gazing, wild and startled, at the approaching train. We were not, however, favoured with this fine picture, or, if it was seen on this occasion, we had our backs turned to it. On our return journey a gentleman pointed out a gorge where he had been with a hunting party, when the horses became restive, and almost unmanageable, without apparent reason, till there was discovered, at some distance, a rattlesnake, which led them speedily to change their quarters.

The sun had set as we were among the mountains, and a large part of the journey was made under the rays of the full moon. But we had to return by the same way, and fortunately did so throughout under bright sunshine. Each experience had its own charm, the moon giving a weird and mysterious effect, concealing much and perhaps exaggerating more, which afterwards appeared in their true and stern grandeur. Both experiences, however, we must seek to blend together, stereoscopically, that we may save repetition.

For upwards of a hundred miles we had been gradually ascending among the hills, till we came to Altoona, which lies in the heart of the mountains, at the base of the steep ascent of the Alleghanies. We rest for a little here, while the railway officials make special preparations for the toilsome way before us. Our train is supplied with two engines; some require three; and a luggage train is waiting to struggle up by the help of four.

The town of Altoona owes its origin entirely to the construction of this railway, and is still chiefly dependent on it and summer visitors, whom it has attracted to the neighbourhood. Five-and-thirty years ago it had no existence, and a single farm occupied the ground. When it was proposed to bring the railway over the Alleghanies, an agent was sent to make a purchase of the farm, and to offer for it fifteen or sixteen hundred pounds. The agent accidentally dropped a note containing these terms; the farmer's wife quietly picked it up, read it, took her husband aside and showed it to him, when the higher price was asked and at once given. The ground thus secured for the Company is now occupied by a town of 25,000 inhabitants, with two daily papers, and all civil and ecclesiastical edifices in harmony. Another spot had been previously purchased by certain speculators who *calculated* that the railway must go their way, on which dwellings were erected, all now left on their hands, a lonely and expensive solitude.

The railway works at Altoona are very extensive, and everything in connection with locomotives is made here, from the first to the finishing touch. It is said that upwards of a hundred engines, and an equal number of passenger cars, with nearly ten thousand luggage waggons, are turned out of the works complete every year. What a marvel among these otherwise lonely mountains! I was pleased to learn that, in its early history, this was an important station on the "underground railway;" that is, it was a stage on the way by which slaves were secretly conveyed from the States, then their house of bondage, to Canada, their land of liberty. The Rev. R. Oliver—a friend of Abraham Lincoln—hid many in his house, and passed them on safely to others; and an active agent in the same work was himself concealed in the Manse for several weeks—John Brown, of Harper's Ferry fame.

Shortly after leaving Altoona we climb up and dive into the Horse, or Colt Shoe, a curve in the railway that sweeps round a deep hollow in the hills. The name may help one to realize the form, but some may do so all the better when we remark that it resembles a railway going up to and round the gorge called the Beef Tub, near Moffat. The turn is a very sharp one, and by no means safe on account of the wild ravine below. An accident occurred here, on the 28th of May last (1887), by which eight persons were killed and six others severely wounded.

Beyond this shoe many a mountain shoulder is encompassed, and many a hollow entered, while we are steadily ascending, sometimes at the rate of 208 feet in the thousand. At one point we may see a train on the edge of a precipice, almost directly over our heads, turning round a sharp corner where the carriages appear twisted and dislocated like a broken back-bone, and are told that there, too, we must go, after making many a winding curve to reach it. At another point we are on an open mountain side, surveying a scene of broad and varied beauty, stretching before us for miles. Or, again, we are looking into gaps and ravines, deep, wild, and dark. In all this diversity of form and elevation, except on the face of some sheer precipice, these mountains are clothed from head to foot with rich forest trees, some of them remnants of the "forest primeval." These ancient and valuable ornaments, however, are rapidly disappearing, not by the wear and tear of the weather, but by the sharp edge of the woodman's axe, wherever he can reach them.

Having, for upwards of a hundred and thirty miles, been passing through an ever-varying scene of hill and vale and rolling river, we have now, for eleven miles more, been toiling up and through these mountains, till we reach our highest point, three thousand feet above the level of the sea. This is called the summit, though only that to which the railway reaches, not that of the range itself. Under the rays of the moon it seemed part of a mysterious dream; but when we afterwards passed it during the day, a broad level space was unveiled all around, with lofty heights still rising above, and glens opening on either side. Here, I understand, a good many years ago, a certain medical doctor took up his solitary quarters, wrote a book in praise of the district, enlarging on the virtues of certain mineral springs near it, and founded a little hotel. "Not," he said, "for wine-bibbers, sensual and profane persons, not for the gross and the godless, not for seekers and lovers of pleasure *alone*, was it to be provided, but for the sick and suffering, the mournful wanderers in the painful world." Now there are two or three enormous hotels, one of them called Mountain House, in architectural beauty, with towers and turrets and surrounding verandas, superior to many a royal palace. In these, and in cottages connected, two thousand guests can be accommodated. I was told by one who resided there for a while, that the climate was so remarkably cool that they sometimes, in summer, required to sleep with blankets on their beds! How often can we anywhere, or at any time, dispense with them?

We toiled up eleven miles to this height by the power of two engines; and thus, according to the laws of the conservation of force and of gravitation, we ought to go down on the other side without any. And so we did. For eleven miles we descended by our own weight,—the engines and brakes being all required to keep us back—with what rapidity or danger we could only faintly realise. Far down, but while still among the mountains, we passed some large blazing coke furnaces, sending forth a strange wild glare by no means in harmony with the surroundings. We must not complain, however, of this. These were but small disfigurements compared with the extent of natural beauty and variety which followed us on this route. During most of the journey, not only when we were crossing the lofty heights, but for a hundred and sixty miles, stretching on either side of the Alleghanies, we were never away from the sight of hills or mountains, with flowing streams or broad rivers. In fact, all the way from New York, for fully 440 miles, we had little that might be called tame, and everything enabled us to realise that Pennsylvania—the wooded land of Penn—did not belie its sweet euphonious name.

After leaving the last station before reaching Pittsburg, the night was far advanced, and Dr. Taylor was alone reading in the parlour, when a man suddenly entered the room from the platform without, and asked if he might hide beneath the sofa, as he could not pay his fare to the city. At the unexpected appearance the doctor felt a little *eerie*, but insisted on the man remaining outside; and to prevent further intrusion, fastened the door from within. Immediately before arriving in the city the intruder quitted his post as suddenly as he had occupied it. He must have leapt on the car and left, when the speed was pretty well up, as he would doubtless have been discovered had he done so near either of the stations. We wonder if such daring practices, for saving or other purposes, are not uncommon at home as well as in America, though there may not always be the same opportunity of detecting them. One case, at least, occurred lately in the North of England, where a robbery and double murder had been committed, and two of the murderers sought to escape their pursuers by getting under a carriage, between the wheels, and lying concealed during a long journey. How uncomfortable for our brother to imagine that such a companion had attempted to join him when alone in the midnight hour!

The approach to Pittsburg, and our entering into it, were revealed by lights stranger far than burning coke furnaces. Flames were seen rising here and there, as if they came directly out of the earth—which in reality they did—and lofty pipes appeared above certain works, with brilliant lights issuing from them, streaming like long narrow banners of fire waving in the breeze. This was the superfluous natural gas, allowed, or requiring to escape, when the works were closed, where it was used for heating their boilers or furnaces. We saw afterwards a broad plate of fire floating on the river like a golden shield, which we supposed to be a similar escape. A newspaper was handed to me where I was told I would find some notice of natural *gas*, when, unfortunately, my eye first caught a report of the speeches of some local representatives, and, in my simplicity, I asked if that was the reference, at which I had to submit to a rebuke for my want of respect for American eloquence.

From this paper, and other sources, I obtained information on the subject that was to me altogether a marvellous revelation. Something like this gas was, no doubt, heard of before, such as the burning spring which we looked into at Niagara. But this was apparently extinct when we were there, and, at best, had been very trifling and fitful in its manifestations; while others are equally rare and useless curiosities. But here, at Pittsburg, is a great power, in wide-spread and active operation, of enormous manufacturing and domestic value. Numerous "wells," as they are called—occasionally fully 2000 feet deep—have been sprung in the district, and in the country around, far and near, where the supply appears simply inexhaustible. Some of these wells have been open for two or three years, since 1884, when the discovery began to come into general use, and they are giving no signs of slackened energy: in several instances the pressure is rather increasing, so that escape pipes are required all around from which flames are constantly issuing day and night.

The gas has no smell, and, when digging for it, its presence is often discovered only by serious explosions, sending the boring instruments into the air, accompanied by a noise like the bursting of a boiler, with a long terrific roar. In such cases it is no easy matter for the men to escape and ultimately seize the hidden monster and lead him in the way of usefulness. The gas is now employed, I understand, in all the various processes of iron, steel, glass, and other manufactures. It is more cleanly than coal—or rather is free from all uncleanness—yields more heat, makes the metal of better quality, is more economical, requires fewer men in the works, saves in fuel more than fifty per cent., and is much less severe on the machinery. It is adopted in hotels and private houses throughout the city, where stoves and grates are being prepared for it in all directions, and where every room is heated, and the cooking in the kitchen entirely accomplished by it; though in these it has not yet been used, to any extent, for illuminating purposes. What a saving all this must be to the work and appearance of domestic servants! And what a vast improvement it has already wrought in the look, and the outlook, of the smoky city! It need no longer bear that grim name, by which it has been most appropriately designated; and that of *Pitchburg* also, by which it was sometimes described, has lost its humour and meaning; for it has now an atmosphere purer far than any of our English manufacturing towns, and it may soon be as sweet as those where furnaces are unknown, though these have hitherto been its most striking features.

On our first visit to Pittsburg, the full moon was struggling with the numerous fiery jets, and blazing banners, to brighten the city, and one could scarcely say which excelled. But, on our return, the morning sun made all other lights 'shine dead,' and revealed, free from any obscuring medium, various fine buildings and public works within; with villas and country seats in the neighbourhood, situated on bold and terraced banks, rising suddenly, and to a considerable height, above the river.

And this is emphatically *the* river—the great Ohio—next to the Missouri furnishing the most abundant supplies for the Mississippi, and thus ranked as one of the notable three! We are looking here at its origin, at the point where its familiar name begins by the junction of two streams, the Alleghany and Monongahela, between which Pittsburg stands.

When we passed through the city, at midnight, one of Dr. Taylor's sons, who is in business there, came to the station, at considerable inconvenience, to give us a kindly greeting—to be ready to receive whom the affectionate father had been keeping vigils, when the unexpected stranger, previously referred to, suddenly appeared. I had followed Mr. C. Taylor from his childhood, and it was interesting to find him here occupying a most promising position in carrying on the important manufacture of steel, one of the great staples of America. It is the place, and the occupation, in connection with which Mr. Carnegie, the Dunfermline boy, amassed his great fortune. May our young friend be not less truly successful and useful than the millionaire! Our intercourse with him, at this time, was brief but refreshing. Soon after, amid thoughts of these blazing lights we had left behind, and the wonderful resources which a Faithful Creator has long been treasuring up for the use of man beneath the earth, and the infinitely more precious resources He has been treasuring up for him above the heavens, we were lulled to sleep by the rattling wheels and trembling car.

CHAPTER XII.

To Chicago.

DAYBREAK had appeared when we passed through Columbus, and found ourselves in the State of Ohio. There was no time to inspect the city, and a glance at the portion within view of the railway station was all we could obtain. It is the capital of the State, and worthy of that dignified position, if being as large as Paisley can be considered sufficient warrant for ruling over a district larger than all Scotland. Here we obtained the morning news, and found our progress, and appearance in these quarters, among the various items. It was stated that Mr Hammond was on his way to Indianapolis with certain guests, whose names were given, but need not be repeated; though it might be flattering to notice the unexpected honours that were attached to some of them.

The natural features of the portions of Ohio

and Indiana, through which we passed, have left a very vague impression on my mind. I can think only of the luxury of private fellowship, or lounging on the easy chair, as vast plains, dotted with small farms, clumps of trees, and brown fields, rapidly opened up, and gradually died away in the distance.

We reached Indianapolis early in the forenoon, after having travelled more than nine hundred miles at a stretch. Here we were met by the Rev. Dr. J. M'Leod, of the Presbyterian Church, who was acquainted both with our host and Dr. Taylor. While Mr. Hammond, whose line of railway is connected with the city, was attending to business, we were kindly entertained in Dr. M'Leod's hospitable manse, with his genial family. The church, with the manse close beside it, is situated at the corner of a large square surrounded by fine private residences, and its lofty spire and noble proportions, not inferior to our home city churches, have ample justice done them. Dr. M'Leod drove us through the principal parts of the city, especially its residential quarters, where we found villas in every style of architecture, all displaying excellent taste. The streets were broad, shaded by splendid trees, behind which the houses were seen richly embowered; the quantity of foliage exceeding anything I had as yet seen, but which I found a growingly prominent feature as we went westward. I have heard of a rustic remarking that Glasgow would be a fine city if it was only in the country. Much of the combination of these apparently opposite excellencies may be found in many American cities, and that of Indianapolis in particular. The streets were abundantly strewn with autumn leaves, as from a forest, and youths were busy enjoying themselves gathering them into heaps and setting them on fire. I remarked that, apart from the unsavoury odour thus sent forth, this was a great waste, for there was no better manure than decayed leaves. "Manure!" said our friend, "why, we have two or three feet of fine black mould all around the city, and need nothing of that." It may be so, but if everything is taken out and nothing put in, even such wealth of soil may be exhausted, as we found in some parts of Canada. Surely the rich, as well as the poor, should learn to "gather up the fragments, that nothing be lost."

Mr. Hammond invited a pleasant party of friends to dine at the hotel, and a greater gathering met afterwards, by the power of attraction, in the private rooms which he had secured. Most of the gentlemen present were in business, or it might be in offices in the city, and all of them cordial and intelligent, talking freely of men and things. A knock came to the door, when one answering it was asked outside, and returned, intimating that a reporter was anxious to interview Dr. Taylor; which request, with a smile, was politely refused. No offence was meant, and none was taken, but no one seemed desirous to have private fellowship, or private opinion, made a matter of public gossip. We had similar experience elsewhere.

We may notice that Mr. H. W. Beecher was minister in Indianapolis for eight years, from 1839 to 1847, when his preaching was of the thoroughly evangelical type which he had been taught in his New England home, and when he showed a thoroughly evangelistic spirit. His first charge was at Lawrence, in the southern extremities of this State.

Our visit to Indianapolis was a most delightful one, and it was late in the evening before we left it. We returned to our car to find again sweet slumber in our berths, above the monotonous music of the wheels. By the time we awoke we were sweeping along the shores of Lake Michigan, whose waters presented an apparently boundless expanse, stretching, as they do, northward to a distance of some three hundred miles. We were now in the State of Illinois, and soon found the houses of Chicago lining our way on the one side, while we were touching the very lip of the lake on the other. It was during a wild gale, with drenching showers, that we entered the great central city of the New World. Had the wind been from the north we might have seen fresh water billows breaking on the shore; but it was from the south, and the lake seemed only as if violently swept with a rude brush. The trees, however, were lashed into fury, and, as we found afterwards, many of their branches, small and great, were torn off and strewn on every path. There was much of home in all this, apart from the trees, reminding us of familiar experiences around our cottage by the sea.

Quarters were secured for us in the Grand Pacific Hotel, one of the most spacious and splendid even in America. It is built of stone, six storeys high, and with length and breadth in proportion, the interior arrangements being such as could scarcely be surpassed. In the morning, though the elements were still unfavourable for seeing much of Chicago, nothing was lost. We were early on the move, some of us going first to a Conference of Congregational ministers assembled from all parts of the States. The large church was well filled, in the area with ministers, and in the galleries with friends and visitors, having very much the appearance of an Assembly or Synod in Scotland. This was all the more realised when I was introduced to several of the brethren, among them to the pastor of the church in which the meeting was held, and who had been speaking, with great effect, when we entered, evidently giving the opening address. His language was clear and natural, without the formality of the paper, or even of the written style, direct, and pointed. He urged the necessity of greater zeal in the cause of the Master, comparing the Church, in a low spiritual condition, to the beach in a bay off the ocean, at ebb tide, covered with tangled weeds;

whereas the Church which enjoyed an abundant outpouring of the Spirit of God was like the same beach filled with the flowing tide, when all was beauty above, and order and harmony beneath.

We listened to one or two other speakers uttering a few pithy words on the duty of congregations to meet the wants of the immigrants constantly pouring into the country, to assist the coloured people, to win the Indians in their neighbourhood to the Saviour, and to preach the gospel among the heathen abroad. It was most refreshing to learn that all the departments of Christian enterprise were carried on so vigorously by the Congregationalists of America, and that the demands of the home field, though most urgent, did not lead them to slacken their zeal for the foreign field. Our stay at the Conference was short, and I could willingly have remained much longer, but I felt, with my fellow-traveller, Mr. Bates, that we had much to see elsewhere, and time was limited.

Immediately on leaving this meeting we were caught in a shower, and, hearing sacred music, were attracted for shelter into, what turned out to be, a Jewish Synagogue. It was a large building, beautifully decorated, and attended by nearly a hundred people, who had shown their interest by leaving their business at mid-day for praise, prayer, and reading of the Scriptures. We listened to a small choir singing in the gallery, with clear melodious voices, and assisted by a powerful organ. They were responding to the minister from the pulpit, who was reading, or rather chanting, from the Hebrew Psalter. The whole service led us to think of Ancient Israel, as they were wont to answer each other in Psalms by the Red Sea or on Mount Zion. It was with a feeling of mingled sympathy and pity that we looked on this fragment of the "tribes of the wandering foot and weary breast," sighing, rather than singing these "songs in the night:" so far from the land of their fathers, and yet so near the truth and Christian influence.

As we had found, in the churches, shelter from frequent showers, so we did in some of the magnificent public buildings, chiefly in the City Hall, and Custom House, and Post Office; and in witnessing the mad contentions in the Stock Exchange. We made the circuit of the city in the cable cars, which pass through the great business quarters; and walked along the principal business streets, though sometimes not without difficulty on account of the storm. On one occasion I saw a hat careering before the gale, and found my friend and fellow-traveller in full pursuit, amid the crowd of men and vehicles, that he might not be left without a covering.

There is nothing in these streets of the mushroom character we are ready to associate with a city that has, once and again, seemed to spring up as in a night. The buildings are of stone, or beautifully coloured brick; not unsightly masses whose only object is accommodation for business, but constructed with considerable architectural taste. We were particularly struck with the enormous warehouses that were being erected on the site of what had evidently been inferior ones. They were already towering seven or eight storeys high, having strong iron supports, with hollow wedge-shaped bricks which we saw the workmen ingeniously fixing together as flooring—all these materials being employed that the structures might be fire-proof. As 'burnt bairns dread the fire,' so do these citizens of Chicago. Hence they have almost entirely renewed the city since the great fire—even those portions of it that escaped—making it much more substantial and safe than it was formerly.

There is one building, however, of considerable interest, which it is well they have preserved, and which was pointed out to us as marking the spot where the great calamity was stayed. It stood almost untouched, when the flames were raging all around and at its portals; and looked out afterwards on a wilderness of blackened ruins, where lately so many hundred happy homes had stood. It was truly a 'brand plucked from the burning.'

The fire of 1871, must ever be memorable, not only in Chicago but in history, as probably the most extensive that ever occurred in any city, not excepting Rome or London. After doing its work of destruction on one side of the river, it crossed, under the influence of a strong breeze, to the other, when altogether four square miles of houses were consumed, and about a hundred thousand persons rendered homeless; the flames being quenched at last, not by the labour of man, but by the drenching showers of heaven. Not less memorable than the fire itself are the promptitude, zeal, and courage with which the ruins were repaired; a work commenced while the embers were still burning, and consummated in a few years. But perhaps most noteworthy of all was the liberality manifested by Christians throughout the States, and in all parts of the world, to help the homeless.

> "Men said at vespers: 'All is well!'
> In one wild night the city fell;
> Fell shrines of prayer and marts of gain
> Before the fiery hurricane.
>
> Ah! not in vain the flames that tossed
> Above that dreadful holocaust:
> The Christ again has preached through thee
> The Gospel of humanity."

We drove to the Water-works, one of the sights of Chicago. The supply is brought from the Lake by a tunnel carried into it for about two miles, so that the opening may be beyond the impurities found nearer the shore. Through this tunnel the water is drawn by most powerful engines, and raised to the top of a tower, about 160 feet high, whence it is distributed by pipes throughout the city. We inspected the engines, and cannot remember ever seeing anything of the kind superior to them, so massive and yet so beautiful. We ascended the tower, and had a complete command of the city; which however, presented nothing picturesque or striking, as it lies on a low level plain, part of a great prairie. But its extent is remarkable, stretching for five miles in every direction, some of its streets being about seven miles long.

In the neighbourhood of the Water-works we drove through some five parks, joined together, and embracing boulevards which alone extend for three miles and a-half. The parks themselves are very extensive, and bear such honoured names as Lincoln, Humboldt, and Garfield; and there are fair attempts in them to relieve the monotony of the flat shores by raising mounds like little hills, interspersed with small streams, bridges, and miniature lakes.

The rapid progress of Chicago is often noticed as an unique feature. It is now a city of 600,000 inhabitants; exactly, by the way, what is calculated as having been that of ancient Nineveh, and only a little short of that of the second city in Britain. Although in the centre of a great continent, it has commercial advantages seldom surpassed. Railways diverge from it in all directions, and it has most extensive water communication. It is linked to all the great lakes of America; and, with assistance of canals, can reach the Atlantic by the St. Lawrence or by the Hudson; and is connected with the Gulf of Mexico by the Mississippi. There is no such inland water communication to be found anywhere in the world. Yet, fifty-seven years ago, this central city had but seventy inhabitants. The first white man who built a house, and resided there, died only the other day. I met two gentlemen who said they knew him well. His name was *MacKenzie*, a genuine Scotch Highlander, who was spared to see his lonely log hut surrounded by innumerable palatial buildings and a teeming population. I remember, when the account of the battle of Alma reached this country, it was noticed that the first post occupied beyond it was MacKenzie farm; and the *Times'* reporter paused, in his brilliant account of the battle, to say—" A Scotchman here too ! "

The dynamite scare had not quite left the city when we visited it, although the most guilty parties were lying then, as they are lying still, condemned to death; and, I suppose, they are likely to remain under that sentence till it is executed in the ordinary course of nature. Attempts, it was feared, would be made to effect the escape of the murderers, and things were said to be very unsettled and unsafe, so that some were doubtful about our venturing out at night. But the darkness is almost turned into day in the great thoroughfares. The electric lights seem here as powerful, and as extensively used, as in New York, if not more so. Hence, without any anxiety, we strolled through the streets, and witnessed some very fine effects, such as that on the tower of the

City Hall, which had a beautiful corona, or chain of electric diamonds, sparkling near its top, and shedding a pleasing radiance all around.

It must be acknowledged that there is much moral and spiritual darkness in the "Garden City of the Lakes." The worst features of European Socialism and Infidelity have settled on it. The criminal classes, also, have sought refuge here in the hope that their antecedents would remain undiscovered in the midst of such a mixed population, gathered together so recently from all quarters, and growing so rapidly, that nearly all are alike strangers, and could not be expected either to give or to ask certificates of character. But the efforts to spread a pure Gospel, in every corner, have been great in proportion to the necessities. There are within its boundaries some three hundred churches, most of them evangelical, with numerous religious institutions of all kinds, and bands of faithful workers, whose combined labours have not been without success. It has sometimes been said, "Why does not Mr D. L. Moodie remain in his own city, when so much has yet to be done, instead of wandering over the world?" Mr Moodie has done a great work in Chicago, personally, and by stirring up and organising others. He knows, however, that his strength is not to sit still, but to diffuse the materials which, with an evangelist, must ever be limited, and also to gather something new for home by going abroad. The Conference of Christian ministers we witnessed in the city, manifesting the most resolute determination to meet the evils by which they are surrounded, and the assurance that the same spirit prevails among all the denominations, may well lead one to cherish hopeful views for the future of this most remarkable centre of population.

CHAPTER XIII.

To the Mississippi.

IT was not without difficulty that we found our way through the intricacies of the upper storeys of the Pacific Hotel, Chicago, to the breakfast table. The corridors run round the building, with numerous passages going inwards, all lined with bed-rooms undistinguishable from each other. We might be able to tell how many storeys we were up from the numbers marked on our keys, as every additional hundred indicated an additional storey; but on which side was our elevator, or into which recess we must go to find it, were questions that could only be answered by experiments, as no one seemed on the move so early in these upper quarters to guide us.

After losing some time and patience, and afraid that we might lose our breakfast or our train, all ended satisfactorily, and we were at length ready for another stage in our journey. It was delightful to be again seated in our easy chairs, looking out from the crystal parlour of our travelling car, waiting for fresh experiences, amid the enjoyment of former fellowship. It was like being once more at home, after spending a day and a night among strangers. But it was some time after starting before we were clear of all signs of the nearness of a great city. We glided on while engines, carriages, and waggons lined the way apparently for miles. This, perhaps, more than anything we had seen, gave us an idea of the vast resources of Chicago, of the extent of its traffic, and of the numerous territories it must reach and influence by its commercial enterprise.

In an hour or so, however, we were far on the boundless prairie, rapidly pushing forward to the West, on our way to Milwaukee. The morning opened with freshness and beauty after the storm of the previous day. There was "the clear shining after the rain." A sweet fragrance seemed to come to us, either from the fields, or flowers, or little clumps of trees we passed now and again. The forests, with which we had been so long familiar in the Eastern States, had gone; and what there was of wood appeared of artificial planting, it might be to relieve the eye, or to afford shelter to the farms which were occasionally coming into view. With the exception of these, the horizon for many miles was unbroken. Yet there was no sense of weariness or monotony. The novelty of the scene prevented that, recalling early story and romance, with songs and dreams of prairie life. We did not, indeed, see much, if anything, here, of primeval grass, so famous for its flowers and fires. Yet that grass abounded only a few years ago, and the flames of its burning had been seen raging with all the fury, and more than the destruction of a hurricane, immediately before the great fire in Chicago.

As we swept swiftly and smoothly over the vast plains, with few windings and no gradients, there were signs of cultivation all along, near the line of railway. Many of the fields appeared small, with a good deal of the cabbage-garden character about them. The farmers or servants were rarely seen, perhaps because they were few, or their autumn work was over, and they were engaged with indoor duties. Almost the only signs of life we witnessed were in the children, singly or in happy groups, with books and bags in hand, proceeding to school. There were no villages in view as centres of education, and cities were far away. Even earth roads could not be discovered. The railway seemed to be their only highway; and we could look for a moment into their bright faces and admire their neat and tidy attire, as they stood aside to let us pass. Was there amongst them another "Rosalea, the prairie flower?" How long they lingered in our view, till their tiny forms died away in the distance! and I thought of the time within the memory of some of their fathers when the wild Indians, before the white man had been seen, hunted the buffalo and the antelope over these vast plains. Many of the sights of that morning's ride have entirely gone from me, but these school children seem still moving on, gathering the blessings of Christian civilisation, and bearing with them the hopes of a great future. Well has Whittier said :—

> "We crossed the prairie, as of old
>   The pilgrims crossed the sea,
> To make the West, as they the East,
>   The homestead of the free !
>
> We go to plant her common schools
>   On distant prairie swells,
> And give the Sabbaths of the wild
>   The music of her bells."

Entering the State of Wisconsin, we reached Milwaukee about mid-day. This was one of the American cities of which I had formed a very vague and most erroneous conception. I thought it was a small lumber town ; that is, one chiefly engaged in the timber trade. Instead of this, however, I found we were in a city considerably larger than Aberdeen, with many and varied industries, and extensive shipping communications with all the Lakes. Our friend, Mr. Hammond, knowing the ground well, took us a drive to the principal sights. The business parts of the city were not inferior to what we had seen elsewhere, and the outskirts were in many respects superior. The esplanade, which overlooks the Lake, unlike that of Chicago, is on the ridge of a steep lofty bank, commanding a bay that sweeps in a graceful curve for several miles, terminating in sharp and pleasing headlands, and is said to resemble that of Naples. The fine residences, rising on the green lawns above the cliffs, embowered in woods and fragrant with flowers, may, indeed, remind one of the Italian city. But Michigan, unlike the Mediterranean, is "an islandless sea," with no bold Capri or Ischia to break the horizon beyond, and no Vesuvius behind.

By a zig-zag road we reach the shore for the purpose of inspecting the Waterworks. Though these are not so large as those of Chicago, the engines are massive and in magnificent order, and sufficiently powerful to raise an abundant supply of water over the heights to the entire city beyond. Dr. Taylor, noticing the strong built frame and dark crisp hair of the engineer, suggested that he must be a Scotchman. We ventured to ask, when he said—"No; but the head is." We were quite satisfied with the mistake when it led to such a reply. The subordinate was a German.

From the heights above it was strange to see a steamer far off on the horizon, and a large vessel, in full sail, seeking the harbour. We could scarcely imagine that it was a fresh water lake on which we were looking, lately paddled only by the Indian canoe. Others seem to have had the same difficulty; for the Americans tell of a vessel, with a British captain and crew, becalmed on the lake, and enduring all the pangs of thirst; failing to remember, or realize, the abundant supply for their wants by which they were surrounded. And are there not many thirsting, or perishing for lack of a more precious fountain, when it is so near that they have only to stoop down and drink?

Milwaukee was interesting in its business quarters: but in this respect it was largely a repetition of the other cities of the West. I was particularly pleased, however, with some of the outskirts, where we found fine villas, built in succession on gently sloping green lawns—fresher than any I had seen in the East or South—which were often cut into graceful flower beds, with fancy shrubs. All these were close on the streets, and without any fence whatever, or only occasionally a slight one to mark the boundary, but not meant to protect the property. The proprietors evidently trust the people, and this confidence even the children do not seem to abuse, as we saw message boys and others playing on the pavements without touching the flowers or grass. Might it not be well if our people were trained after the same manner? Trust might in the end bring greater safety than attempts to exclude. These villas, and most of the houses of Milwaukee, are built of fine cream-coloured bricks, which have a pleasing effect, and have given to it the name of the Cream City of the Lakes.

I was not surprised to learn that Scotch

gardeners often find their way to this city as furnishing a fit sphere for their labours; and I knew one, at the very head of his profession, who, with his family, lately settled there. The climate suits them, the element of cold, which, on the whole prevails, being more congenial than heat; its scenery pleases them, for, though neither mountainous nor even hilly, it is by no means flat; and its soil yields richly to the zeal and care to which they have been trained in the more stubborn regions of their native land. Our farmers also may well be attracted to this neighbourhood. Ground, however, may be much more easily obtained further north, toward Manitoba; and the prominence of the German element in Milwaukee—probably two-thirds of the entire population—is to some a serious drawback.

We returned to our car in the evening and set out for Minneapolis. Knowing that about the dawn we would reach the Mississippi, I was anxious to see it with the first opportunity, and asked Mr Johnson to "wake me early." Faithful to his promise, and whilst I was still locked in slumber, our coloured friend drew aside the curtain, and roused me with the information that we had come to the scenery. After a struggle to open my eyes, lying still, with scarcely a turn of the head, I looked out on a picture fairer far than my dreams. The eastern horizon was tinged with golden indications of the coming day. The roseate hue was shading into orange, as the eye followed it upwards, till it melted in the deep blue; and the morning star, brighter than ever I had seen it before, burned like a lamp on the border where the blue and the orange met. The banks were lined with brushwood, intermixed with lofty trees; one of which lifted itself up into the dawn, when every branch and twig, stript of their leaves by the autumn frosts, could be clearly traced, relieved on the golden light, while the whole was reflected on the quiet silver stream beneath. No circumstances could be more favourable in which, for the first time, to behold the great Father of Waters. The picture is photographed in my memory in every detail—I could almost say for life.

How long I gazed lovingly on the sight, without lifting my head from the pillow, I cannot say. But it suddenly occurred to me that the motion of our car had ceased, and that the scene had been all the while a stationary one. I felt it strange that we should be waiting in such a lonely solitude; somewhat as the passengers feel when the screw of the vessel stops in mid-ocean. And there was reason for alarm. On rising I learned that scarcely had Mr. Johnson awakened me, when danger signals appeared, indicating that something was wrong before us; and hence the stoppage. Then it was remembered that an express was coming rapidly behind, on our single line; and the guard had gone back with torpedoes, and had just returned breathless, in the hope that a terrible collision would be averted. I looked behind, and there was the engine of the express, close at hand. But it was coming gently up, its speed had been slackened in time, and we were safe. After some further delay, and moving slowly till we passed the partially wrecked waggons that had been dragged aside, we hastened on our journey; all the more grateful to the Gracious Preserver that a danger had been realized and yet escaped.

Our line now lay alongside the Mississippi, or at no great distance from it, for about a hundred miles, and the scenery was on the whole picturesque. We had crossed the river, and were within the State of Minnesota, making our way for Minneapolis, and expecting to turn aside and see Minnehaha. But why so many *misses* and *minnies* in this region? Besides those we have mentioned there are still more to be encountered. Both words are of the same significance, and, in the language of the Sioux Indians, mean *water*. Mississippi, is the father of waters; Missouri, the muddy waters; Minnesota, the sky-blue water; Minnehaha, the laughing water; and Minneapolis is an unnatural compound of tongues, whose people never knew each other—the Roman and the Indian—and signifies the city of waters. All the names are remarkably appropriate, and the whole State of Minnesota is the fountain from whence some of the greatest rivers of the world take their rise. We have the Red River—the principal feeder of Lake Winnipeg, which connects with Lake Superior and all the others of the great chain—flowing on toward the north-west till it reaches the Gulf of St. Lawrence; and the Mississippi—which is fed by innumerable lakes and swamps, some say nearly a thousand—flowing on toward the south till it reaches the Gulf of Mexico. The sources of these two rivers are only a few miles apart, so that, in floods, their waters sometimes intermingle, while their mouths are nearly three thousand miles apart. May we suggest that Minnesota, both from its name and its nature, is a clear case of Hydrocephalus?

We reached Minneapolis in time for a hotel breakfast. After driving through the principal streets of the city—not behind many of those in our own country in business, and exceeding them in breadth—we set out to visit the falls of Minnehaha, which Longfellow has made so famous through his "Hiawatha." They are a few miles from the city, and reached by a beautiful country road, not unlike what we have often seen among the hills and dales of Scotland. There is, properly speaking, only one fall, coming, in a broad silver sheet, over a shelving rock, amid rich woods, and breaking at a considerable depth below, with more of the noise of a great shower than of a cataract. The water is projected a considerable distance from the rock, and falls like the "big rain that comes dancing to the earth!" Hence, perhaps, the name Minnehaha. How often the poet repeats it, and revels in its sweet significance!

> "In the land of the Dacotas,
>   Where the Falls of Minnehaha
> Flash and leap among the oak-trees,
>   Laugh and leap within the valley."

Here dwelt the Indian arrow maker, and

> "With him dwelt his dark-eyed daughter,
>   Wayward as the Minnehaha;
> And he named her from the river,
> From the water-fall he named her,
>   Minnehaha, Laughing Water."

We observed two gentlemen proceeding, not to the fall, but behind it. So two of us followed their example, and found a path worn in the rock, with firm footing, where we could stand and look out on the stream passing over our heads, and plunging, or apparently hanging before us, as a crystaline and semi-transparent veil. We crossed over to the other side by this path, and looked again at the happy waters beneath, losing themselves amongst the woods. But we must confess, however deeply we were interested in it, we did not think the scene, as a whole, worthy of the praises and the prominence given it by the poet, in what is, in many respects, his most popular and original work, where the mythical and real are so charmingly blended. Perhaps it was somewhat marred to us by the unshapely wooden erections that have been placed on the fine point of view immediately opposite, intended for refreshments and the sale of fancy Indian work; and, also, by the ground being trampled and bared by the crowds which visit it from the neighbouring cities of Minneapolis and St. Paul. From these places both trams and trains come, at certain seasons, with large pic-nic parties. Yet why should we think poetic or picturesque scenes spoiled because multitudes are permitted, and have the taste, to enjoy them? Surely something of amenity may well be sacrificed for their sakes.

On our way to Minnehaha we turned aside into a suburban district that was being formed into a Public Park. After we had experienced, for a while, the sensation of sailing along in our cab over the waving earth roads, our horse climbed up and over steep heights, where roads of any kind were altogether unknown, and the ground was full of swelling undulations. Here the noble animal twisted and turned as if it had nothing to drag behind it, while we tossed about as in an ocean storm. We were amply rewarded, however, by the fine panoramic view of the city and country around, which we obtained from the summit. Though destitute of the back ground of mountain or lake, there were fine knolls and downs in all directions, relieved by the waters of the Mississippi, as they were seen gleaming,

o

now and again, between their steep banks. The selection of this spot, as the central one for a park, shows the enterprise and excellent taste of these new settlers in the North West, and that they are resolved not to be behind their older and wealthier neighbours in the East in providing the means of recreation and healthy enjoyment. Nor are they behind them in providing the means of religious and mental instruction, as they have upwards of seventy churches—many of whose beautiful spires we saw from the suburban height—with a University and Museum, containing together about 30,000 volumes.

A prominent object here, and in the landscapes of the West generally, near the cities, is the Elevator. By this you must not understand a machine by which you can be raised from storey to storey of a building, but a huge building itself, by which grain is raised to great heights for storage, and as an invaluable aid in transferring its treasures wherever these may be required. The lower portion has numerous flats, raised as high as most people would consider safe; yet there is a portion above this, raised as high again, but tapering somewhat, that the centre of gravity might not be in a position positively and obviously dangerous. The Elevators of Minneapolis are largely supplied with grain from the districts around Lake Superior and Manitoba, with which there is easy and speedy communication by rail. Any one of these is a veritable cornu-copia. But, in endeavouring to make them contain as much golden treasure as possible, all beauty is sacrificed to bulk. It is so also with the numerous imitations we find rising up in the old country. Fortunately, however, we have not so much beauty to mar near those cities where our elevators are beginning to be seen; and I am not aware that they ever appear so gigantic with us as in America. The largest we saw in the North-west is known as the St. Anthony Elevator, in which an unfortunate fire took place, in July last, (1887), when upwards of five hundred bushels of wheat were destroyed.

The principle on which they are wrought is very simple. The grain, as it arrives, is raised by machinery to the storey that may be most convenient for receiving it; and then, when required, it is allowed to pour forth, by the law of gravitation, in a continuous stream, led by a pipe, or other duct, to the waggon or boat to be loaded. The time occupied in filling even the largest of these is marvellously short, measured not by hours but by minutes.

We paid a visit to the mills of Minneapolis, and were permitted to inspect one in full operation—the most extensive in a group of more than a score, and said to be the second largest in the world. It is situated, as are all the others, close to the Falls of St. Anthony, where water power is provided by the Mississippi, having advantages which, I suppose, cannot be surpassed. The river, at this part, is as broad as the Thames at London, flows rapidly, is never dry or low, has a fall which renders all dams unnecessary, and scarcely requires any lades to lead it to its work, or only those of the simplest kind.

Looking out on the waters, from a lofty storey in the mill, the view was very fine, in spite of the fact that the buildings, on either bank, presented little else than enormous food-making factories. The long line of white foam, neither artificial nor uniform, but beautifully broken into two portions, that looked askance on each other, lost little of natural loveliness by the surroundings, and seemed happy in helping to grind food for the millions. No artist, seeking to sketch the Falls, would altogether regret the presence of these mills, standing in various positions, with the curious buildings connected with them jutting out on crags and corners; while the noble suspension bridge, and the city, with its spires and church towers, form the distance.

I cannot venture to describe minutely the interior of the great flour mill, and the marvellous machinery there; for much of it I failed to understand. But I must notice, briefly, some of its leading features. The process of grinding is by iron or steel rollers, with spiral grooves—stones being very little used, and that only for an early process. The grain is carried by endless belts to the eighth floor, where its troubles begin. In its first descent, to nearly the bottom of the mill, the straw and chaff are thrown off, the grains of different sizes separated, and the first slight wounds inflicted. Up again to the top the portions thus prepared are drawn, only to receive more severe treatment between the rollers. Another ascent, and down through the crushing metal it passes, till the heart of each grain is broken. Next, as if kindness were meant, it is gently sifted several times in silken sieves, and fanned, that it might be cooled and cleared. Other upward journeys, and downward crushings follow; the edges of the rollers, between which the grain passes, becoming closer and closer, so that the smallest particle cannot escape the cruel steel. Five such journeys are sufficient for ordinary flour; but sometimes fifteen are taken, till at length nothing is left but the pulverised heart, pure and light as the driven snow.

There was a large portion of one of the lofts occupied with small bags filled with flour, ready for exportation, which had accumulated for a day or two; detained on account of a strike among the switch men on the railway. Most of these bags, we were told, were destined for Glasgow. It was interesting to think that, after travelling over the great continent for more than a thousand miles, and then crossing the ocean, my former fellow-townsmen, and many of my fellow-countrymen, would feed on what both grew and was ground on these uplands of the

Mississippi; and that I might sometimes find supplies coming from the same quarter to my own table. From what we saw, we could faintly realise the vast quantity of flour that must be manufactured in all the mills of Minneapolis. It is said that, besides the local consumption, there is sent out of the country nearly two million barrels; which would make fully five hundred million loaves, or about an annual allowance of half a loaf for every man woman and child on the surface of the globe!

These extensive works, with their superior advantages, have helped greatly to injure the flour mills of Britain: in fact they may be said to have ruined them. Owners and workmen have lately held meetings in Glasgow and elsewhere, at one of which we noticed a speaker declare, that 'no thinking man could stand idly by and see the mills, one by one, becoming silent, and the profits transferred to American purses;' and where resolutions were adopted to petition Parliament to the effect, 'that the time had now arrived when the manufactured products of other nations should bear the same proportion of local taxation as our own.' Sympathy must be felt for the sufferers, while grave doubts may be entertained of the success of these efforts for their protection.

We were shown a portion of the machinery of the great mill at Minneapolis, which has a tragic interest connected with it. It was a fire-proof receiver, into which the finest dust, floating through the mill, was gathered by a process of fanning. This dust is highly inflammable; and, when mixed with air, becomes like gunpowder, or dynamite. An iron nail happened on one occasion to get between the rollers—how this was afterwards known we cannot say—and the friction caused by the rapid motion and crushing made it red hot. In this state it was thrown off the machinery into the dust-room, when the mill became like an ignited bombshell, which instantly burst, and the whole building was blown into fragments. It is said to have been literally annihilated. Not one stone was left upon another; and the ground, where it stood, was torn up as if by an earthquake or volcano, and the machinery buried beneath. Two mills, and an Elevator in the neighbourhood, were levelled in the dust, and other three mills utterly ruined. This awful destruction, however, did not paralyse the industry, but led to its renewal on safer principles; and the fire-proof receiver was invented. By it the danger is reduced to a minimum, if not removed altogether; and what was before such deadly dust is now carefully preserved as valuable food. Thus "out of the destroyer has come forth meat."

CHAPTER XIV.

To Kansas City.

OUR intention was to remain in Minneapolis over the Sabbath, but the strike among the switch men there made it doubtful if we would get away on the Monday. So we started for St. Paul before sun-set on Saturday. This city is about nine or ten miles further down the Mississippi, and the drive to it, in our car, was very interesting. The line goes along the edge of lofty banks above the river, and we looked over these on houses and works far below, built close to the water. We had also a fine view of the cliffs, on the opposite side, on which houses of somewhat curious construction are seen to cling.

In our hotel we met with a gentleman whose presence linked us with our Ayrshire home — Mr. Williamson, a son of the member of Parliament for

Kilmarnock Burghs. He recognized Dr. Taylor, and told us he was on his way from San Francisco. It was worth his while turning aside from the direct course to this charming part of Minnesota, whether business or pleasure was the main inducement. And it furnished us with one of the pleasing surprises of travel —common especially in America—of meeting, both in out-of-the-way places, and in crowded centres, persons whom we may have known more or less intimately.

On Sabbath we had to pass, on our way to church, a great fire which had just broken out in a large warehouse, and which continued to blaze all the day. Such calamities are of frequent occurrence in the States, where so much wood is used in the buildings; and especially at the beginning of their severe winters, when stoves are being kindled. But every preparation is evidently made to meet the danger. The band of firemen we saw, on this occasion, was strong; but I was specially struck with the engines they employed in their work. They were numerous, arriving speedily on the spot, stationed, not only in the street immediately opposite the fire, but at the corners of streets all around. They were small, and wrought by steam, with their boilers and wheels of bright burnished steel; looking more like models than instruments to cope with devouring flames. The steam appeared to be got up on the way; but wood was constantly supplied to sustain it, and great pressure secured. We regretted to learn that two of the firemen perished in the flames they bravely sought to extinguish.

In the morning we worshipped in Plymouth Congregational Church, where, both in regard to forms and doctrine, we felt as if we were in an orthodox Presbyterian Church at home. We had the pleasure of hearing the pastor of the congregation preach, and of afterwards being introduced to him, and several of his deacons and members, to many of whom Dr. Taylor was, at least, well-known by name. The doctor preached in the evening, and the matter having got abroad during the day, there was a large attendance. The church is a very handsome and commodious one, built on a slight elevation, overlooking one of the principal streets. I was delighted to discover, on reading Whittier's poems, since my return to Scotland, that he has one entitled, "Hymn for the opening of Plymouth Church, St. Paul, Minnesota:" and I cannot resist the opportunity of extracting two verses:—

> "No lack Thy perfect fulness knew:
> For human needs and longings grew
> This house of prayer, this home of rest,
> In the fair garden of the West.
>
> O Father! deign these walls to bless;
> Fill with Thy love their emptiness;
> And let this door a gateway be
> To lead us from ourselves to Thee!"

I may here mention that in our hotel there was

a notice, fixed in a most prominent position, containing a list of the churches in St. Paul, with the situation of each mentioned, the ministers' names, and the hours of service. Underneath were the words, "We all are brethren." On this notice I counted the names of seventy-five churches. I find, from the census of 1880, that then there were only forty. The population was at that time fifty thousand, and has, of course, considerably increased since. But surely it must be acknowledged that the proportion of churches, both in regard to population and increase, is most creditable, and a proof of what Christians can do, when all are alike free, and realize their entire responsibility to maintain and extend the cause of Christ.

The general aspect of St. Paul is very pleasing. The business centres are well built, lively, and apparently thriving. But there is a special attraction in the district devoted to private residences. It is a broad lofty ridge overlooking the river, with a noble stretch of vale and wood far beyond; and the houses, varied and chaste in their structure, are ranged along this for about two miles, each dwelling standing apart, shaded in rich foliage, smiling and fragrant with flowers. The cliffs, however, lack the dark weather-beaten appearance, with fern, or moss-grown corners, which make our own so picturesque; and they seemed somewhat new-like in their bare light-grey.

It is at St. Paul, or immediately below the falls at Minneapolis, that the navigation of the Mississippi begins. We saw enormous rafts, above the falls, brought from the great forests of the north. Much of this timber is cut into boards at mills in the neighbourhood; but much also is made to run the rapids, and taken down the river by steamboats, more than two thousand miles, to the sea. The steamboats are curious, I might say comical, structures. Each is propelled by one paddle at the stern, not covered with a box as with us, but fully exposed, and about three-fourths out of the water, like a monster with its tail curled up; and the funnels— generally two—are not arranged from stem to stern, but on opposite sides of the boat, like his tall and slender horns. The rafts are not towed by these steamers, but pushed before them, and sometimes held back when the current is strong. The boats are flat bottomed, and the paddles are high out of the water, because of the numerous shoals to be encountered. The same principle of navigation we observed at Pittsburg, where coals are conveyed on large barges, or rafts, and similarly propelled down the Ohio, to the Mississippi and the sea.

A very extensive commerce is carried on at St. Paul, and is the main source of its wealth; while manufacture is the main source of the wealth of Minneapolis. The two cities, being so near each other, and almost equal in population—each about the size of Greenock—are great rivals. St. Paul is the capital of the State, and has five daily papers, and seventeen weekly ones; in which respect, I suppose, its rival is not much behind it. The American papers, I may remark, even as far west as this, are generally well conducted, containing not only very fully the news of their own country, but much more of ours than we give of theirs. I was amused, however, at the titles, in large letters, sometimes given to European intelligence—"*Old World Worries.*"

When we look at the size, progress, stability, and beauty of these two cities, besides other towns in Minnesota, and remember how lately the whole contained only dense forests, or vast hunting fields for the Indian, we may well be astonished. The first house was built in this wilderness, as a home of the white man, not more than fifty years ago; the first street, to form a little village, was marked out only forty years ago; the American Government purchased some twenty millions of acres in the State from Sioux Indians, as late as 1851; and still these men of the woods have villages near the cities, and occasionally enter them, in all their wildness and original attire.

We left St. Paul on the Monday forenoon. The air was crisp and cold, with indications that the severe winter experienced in these high and central regions, was at hand. The gentlemen appeared in cloaks, trimmed round the neck, and in the front, with broad fur; and the ladies seemed entirely wrapt up in that cozy attire. We noticed that even the hardy men and women from the country, who came to sell their produce, were thoroughly armed, in their own way, against the weather. I was specially amused with the manner in which they sought to protect their fingers and hands, which were encased in woollen mittens, like boxing gloves, with the thumb alone at liberty. Sleighs and toboggans were exposed for sale; and altogether it seemed as if we were in the Arctic regions, and might be caught in all their severity if we did not immediately hasten southward. And yet it was only the 18th of October!

As for ourselves, we were well provided against the cold with an extra supply of greatcoats, being warned of what might possibly come. In the car we had hot water pipes, which distributed the warmth equally through every corner, and could be regulated, from the kitchen, to any temperature. By this means —instead of employing stoves—one of the sources of danger in railway travelling in America was diminished. When accidents occur, especially in winter, there is great risk of the horrors of fire being added to the general crash. It was so, near Springfield, between Albany and Boston, not long after we had been there, as we noticed in its place; and it has been so again, near the same spot, in the month of February, 1887, in connection with an excursion train, crowded with passengers, proceeding to the festivals at Montreal, with yet more disastrous consequences. The blazing stoves, no doubt, contribute to the awful fatality in these cases, along with the oil lamps and kitchen fires; and it was well that in our car a safer, as well as a more comfortable heating apparatus, was used. With these preparations against any injurious effects from its severity, I enjoyed the signs and foretastes of winter, and the nip of the air outside seemed quite to brace me up. But I cannot say how it might have been in mid-winter; as I find, from newspapers on this side, intelligence, dated 4th January, 1887, stating that "the mercury was 36 degrees below zero at St. Paul, Minnesota."

Our course from this city, for several miles, lay along the banks of the Mississippi. These, though not steep, are by no means flat, and a little beyond rise into fine hills and knolls. The river is frequently parted into several branches, forming islands, well wooded, pleasing, and sometimes picturesque. Passing a steep cutting, apparently for a new railway, I noticed, what I had never seen before, a large steam shovel at work, which must be able easily to compete with more than a dozen navvies.

When we left the river, and drove along the plains, we found ourselves crossing the great prairies of the Land of the Dakota, not far from the State which bears that name. These sometimes seemed unbounded as the sea. The horizon was broken only by little wind-mills, close to the line, used to raise water for the engines, and looking, in the distance, like lonely ladies fluttering their fans.

In the midst of the prairies we entered the State of Iowa. The cultivation here was not such as we had found in districts of the same kind between Chicago and Milwaukee, and much of the soil seemed in its primitive state—the natural grass waving in the breeze, but without any signs of the famous flowers. We saw a herd on horseback looking after his cattle; but whether he required to ride on account of the extent of ground over which they had to graze, or the absence of fences, or his distance from home, or the dangers around, we could not say. At all events, he appeared dignified and picturesque, as no cow-herd generally does, realizing to us the Indian amid his uninvaded solitudes, hunting the wild buffalo.

There were long lonely tracts on this journey, with here and there the hut of some solitary settler. Villages were few, and not very large. We came close to one, evidently of very recent origin—its situation probably suggested by the nearness of the railway—consisting of some fifteen wooden houses, newly and brightly painted, with colours varying according to the taste of their owners, set down on a treeless plain, without a bush as yet rising up to shelter them, with no signs of path or earth road between them, but only the fresh cut sward, flat as a bowling green. The whole seemed as if placed on a calm and boundless sea; or like toy houses which a child has arranged on a smooth parlour carpet. It was an easy and simple beginning, compared with the toilsome clearances in the back-woods, but by no means so romantic. It was much more likely, however, to make rapid progress. Yet even here there must be disappointments, sometimes sad ones, in connection with these new settlements. At one point we came close to a few gravestones, forming a little cemetery, far from any village or dwelling, as none could be discovered on all the prairie around. These were, most probably, the graves of a household which once sought to establish a township here; but, failing to gather others around them, had removed to some more hopeful ground, and, as the only trace of their former presence, had left their dead behind them.

The night rapidly drew its curtains over these wide regions, and I drew the curtains, in due course, in front of my little berth. My thoughts, perhaps my dreams, were of these attempts to found new cities on this unpeopled wilderness. I imagined them as, in many respects, a repetition, after fully four thousand years, of the work of a Nimrod, or an Ashur, making a beginning of Babylon and Nineveh, with a few mud or wooden huts, on the plains of Shinar and Assyria; while other foundations, equally hopeful at the time, faded like Jonah's gourd, and have left only names behind. May not history repeat itself still further, so that some promising new Indianapolis or Minnieapolis will end, even with the present generation, only in a Necropolis; and long before the next four thousand years, the most successful cities of the West will have passed away, and their very sites be long lost, as were those of the East? And may not some future Layard be found making diligent search among deserted mounds, and vast heaps of rubbish, for traces of Capitols and Custom-Houses, Churches and Colleges, Exchanges and Elevators, remains of the proud cities of the prairies of Iowa? The picture is just as probable of realization and as pleasing (?) as that of Macaulay's New Zealander on the ruined arches of London Bridge.

Except these dreams, which some of the sights suggested, there was not much particularly attractive on this part of our journey. And I could not help feeling what a weary land this must be to any settled on it, who bore with them the memory of mountains and glens in the lands they had left. The Scotchman does not naturally choose the prairies, but prefers the rugged, though colder, regions of the North. Those reared on the plains of England and Holland, and those from the bogs of Ireland, who can find their way thus far west, may feel quite at home here. As for myself, the charm of crossing such a vast expanse still continued, if with diminished freshness; but it was mainly because I was a stranger passing through it, and not a settler. There is much of Iowa, however, that is well peopled, prosperous, and advanced; but unfortunately these portions were largely hid from us as we rolled onwards in the dark.

When the morning broke we were on the banks of the Missouri. Its waters are here broader and more rapid than those of the Mississippi, where we first encountered it; and it was an agreeable change, from the streamless prairies, to come on this lively flowing river, and gaze, for the first time, on the principal feeder of the great American water course. But the Missouri has not the attractions of its younger companion, being muddy and turbid throughout; and perhaps it may be for this reason, and in contempt, that, though the longer of the two by fully a thousand miles, its name is lost when their waters intermingle.

Here we look across on the State of Kansas, so prominent in connection with the events which immediately preceded the War of Secession. It was then a comparative solitude, where the slave-holders and friends of freedom contended as to who should secure it, and colonize it for their party. Now a large portion of it is well cultivated, and cities are rising up in all its borders.

We spent the day in Kansas City; not, be it observed, situated in the State whose name it bears, though overlooking it, but in that of Missouri. This city must be of very recent origin, as I do not find its name in geography books, or Encyclopædias of twenty years ago. Yet, in 1880, it had a population of 55,000; and I am informed, on good personal authority, that in the autumn of 1887 it had about 120,000. It seemed to us like a house into which an unexpected number of guests was pouring, where all was confusion and bustle, that accommodation might be made for new arrivals; and where every corner, previously put in order, was completely crowded. It is said that a gentleman, who was lately extolling its growth and energy, was asked, "When were you there?" "Last week," was the reply. "Last week? Ah! but you should see it *now!!*"

When we entered it the bustle was marvellous. Driving from the station, there was a complete block, when conveyances of every possible description were jammed together — humble carts, formed of a few rough boards, unpainted and unplaned; lorries and waggons, heavily ladened; buggies, slender and light, as if formed of tender twigs; with cabs and carriages, which were generally supplied with two horses. In some of the principal streets, not unlike Argyle Street, Glasgow, vehicles stood at almost every shop door, while their owners, many of them evidently from the country, were doing business within. "When farmers ride it and doctors foot it," is said to be a Chinese proverb for plenty. We do not know how it is with the doctors in Kansas City, but certainly the farmers meet the condition of the proverb. I was told that horses were very cheap here; that an excellent one might be purchased for some twenty pounds, a good pony for four pounds, while either could be reared in the country for not more than two pounds a year.

Independently of the means of locomotion thus furnished, so cheaply and abundantly, by horse flesh, cable cars are constantly running through the City, and to the suburbs. It is somewhat curious, at first, to see these cars, two, three, and sometimes four, linked together, moving steadily on, as if by magic, without horse, or steam, or any apparent motive power. They are most useful where there is great traffic, either constantly or at certain periods of the day, when an extra supply can be attached; or where there are steep gradients, when the pain and risk to horses and passengers are avoided. We saw one here coming down a very steep incline, in the form of a long wooden bridge over a valley, where no horse could be trusted.

The manner in which the cars are moved and controlled is very simple. Between the rails there is a little open space, extending all the length of the line, under which is the cable of wire, in constant motion, wrought by engines at the two extremities. I happened once to get a glimpse at Brooklyn Bridge, behind, or rather beneath the scene, when I saw an iron hand put down from the front carriage by means of an iron arm, which was constructed so as to grasp the cable under the control of the driver, causing some friction at first, but the hold was firm, and the carriages gradually moved on, and soon at full speed. This arm goes along the opening all the way, and the hold can be let go at any moment, and the carriages brought to a stand-still.

In this employment of cable cars, as in many other things, our American cousins are gradually being copied. Lines, constructed on this principle, have lately been laid down in one of the suburbs of London. Edinburgh, also, is following the example in one of her principal streets, whose steepness is a source of difficulty and danger, and where some serious accidents have occurred to omnibuses. No other Scotch town has hitherto tried the experiment. Yet how common cable cars are in America! I had previously used them in New York, Philadelphia and Chicago, and found them smooth, speedy, and most commodious. They are rapidly becoming the rule in the cities of the West, and are sure to prove a success wherever there is sufficient traffic to give them encouragement.

The good people of Kansas City were not content with what they already possessed of these lines, but were opening up their streets for cable cars in every direction. In the sultry heat of the afternoon we were glad to take advantage of one of them to help us up a hill, though we were little more than five minutes' walk from the hotel, to which we were returning. The change of temperature from St. Paul to this, I may remark, was most marvellous. Inside the hotel the heat was oppressive, and I had to seek coolness by sitting outside on a chair, which I moved, from time to time, to enjoy the shadow of an awning. The journey between the two cities occupied only twenty-four hours. But in that time we had passed through six degrees of latitude, and descended from a considerable elevation.

We drove round the suburbs; and from some of the heights, which form an important feature of the City, we had extensive views of the country around, which was wooded, yet evidently well cultivated. There is a pleasing range of hills beyond, from which, we learned, the water supply is derived. It was a comfort to know that neither man nor beast was compelled to drink of the muddy Missouri. The citizens have evidently great ambition, and are confident of a great future; for, in this neighbourhood, numerous long broad streets are laid out in all directions, though they are as yet only earth roads, over which we proceed in silent but ever surging motion. Fine buildings are rapidly rising all along these; but there are meanwhile many unoccupied sites, where weeds are allowed to grow, with stems as thick as one's wrist, and as tall as one's self. These might be the product of a few months, and serve, or be intended to advertise the wealth of the soil.

The coloured people have a considerable prominence in Kansas City. In some departments they do not excel as workmen, especially where hard toil is expected. I saw some quarrying, who seemed to think that every three strokes of the pick should be rewarded with three minutes' rest or conversation. But they make excellent waiters, and are evidently proud of their profession. We were amused at two in our hotel, whose business it was to brush the clothes of the guests. As they came slap over our shoulders, or backs, with their straw switches, they also gave their hands a turn of the instrument, as if to clean the dust from it, and in doing so played a merry tune; our broad cloth and their black hands being treated as twin kettle drums on which to display their musical talents. The coloured people, too, make good drivers, and we saw many in Kansas with their own conveyances. Occasionally a quiet revenge for the old condition under slavery is taken by a coloured master, who may be seen reclining at ease in his carriage and pair, with his white servant in charge.

CHAPTER XV.

From the West.

FOR about three hundred miles we travelled through the State of Missouri, during the night, and it was early in the morning when we approached St. Louis. A little above the city the two great rivers of America are united. Some rivers, like the blue Rhone and the brown Arve, seem loath to lose their separate characters; and, whilst they unite, yet retain for a time their distinct individuality. But the union here is instantaneous and complete. Unfortunately, however, in this, as in the case of many other unions, the stronger and the more impure imparts its character to the weaker and the sweeter. The muddy Missouri, which has journeyed eight hundred miles longer than the Mississippi, loses indeed its name in that of its companion, but not its nature.

Both are henceforth equally impure, and become growingly so. During the remainder of the journey—some eighteen hundred miles—the joyous life and beauty of youth are gone, a dull and flat existence follows, ending in sad divisions immediately before entering the Great Gulf.

From the large iron—or rather steel bridge—said to be a mile and a quarter long, which crosses the river at St. Louis, we saw the effect immediately produced, in volume and colour, by the meeting of the waters. And from the same point we obtained a hurried, but pleasing view of the city, with the bold broken banks on which it is built. We regret, however, that time did not permit of our visiting in detail the works, and wonders, and beauties that rose up before us; for, next to Chicago, it is the largest city in the Western States, and is more ancient, and in many respects more interesting, than its rival. In population it considerably exceeds Edinburgh, and is not behind it in signs of civilization; but it must yield the palm to the Scottish capital in situation.

We have many indications of the extensive traffic, by river and rail, carried on at St. Louis, and learn that it is one of the greatest emporiums for produce, and for cotton and tobacco. The steamboats are seen in shoals, all with the curious stern paddles, and said to line the quays, or levees as they are called, for more than a mile and a-half. The railway station, where we spent some time, was a scene of extraordinary bustle. Here a plan is adopted of relieving the pressure, not altogether according to our ideas and habits. There is a broad wooden platform, or floor, stretching across the entire line, where numerous trains are arriving or departing, or are lying abreast. Passengers must wend their way amongst these in reaching or leaving their train. And this they may do without danger, at least of stumbling on the rails, as these are not above but on the level of the platform. But other and more serious dangers have to be encountered; which were painfully obvious as we watched individuals, or groups, wandering amongst the labyrinth of trains, sometimes in front of an engine, which was just arriving, or of another, which was just starting. Among those who had to run this gauntlet we observed an old lady—evidently very timorous—with two gentlemen, linked one to each arm, and a coloured porter, with his hand on her back, encouraging her on, saying, 'Come along, mother, come along, it's quite safe." It was a pleasing picture of kindness and gallantry, which I found very common in America. But really one could not be surprised at young ladies as well as old, and men as well as women, requiring an arm or a word of encouragement in venturing so near the wheels, and in the face of moving engines: although the motion might be gentle, and with tolling bells giving intimation of their progress. One of the brethern drew my attention to a train at our side, behind which my name was exhibited in large letters, with the word *Express* attached; and I discovered that it referred to a town in the neighbourhood so named—a favourite resort of the St. Louis merchants, where many of them reside, and travel daily to and from business.

Leaving this beautiful and prosperous city, and with it the waters of the Mississippi, we were once more sweeping over streamless prairie lands. But these were in a high state of cultivation, with orchards and gardens, and fields where the yellow grain was seen piled up in heaps. Quiet farms came into view, where cattle, swine, and poultry abounded. The huge Elevator was also frequently seen, and an occasional coal mine. We were in the State of Illinois, near its Southern extremity, as we had formerly been at its Northern; the two points being about three hundred miles apart. The next State to the South, from whose borders we were not far distant, is Kentucky; reminding us of Uncle Tom's "Heaven is better than Kintuck." But we were going Northward, and could not turn aside to see the negro's land of Beulah.

We made for Springfield, the capital of Illinois. This must not be mistaken for another of the same name, near Boston, where we spent two or three dreary hours about midnight, and where two sad accidents have occurred since. The Springfield of the West is situated on the border between the open prairie and the forest. It has many excellent buildings which rise above the plain, and are seen from afar; conspicuous among which is the Capitol, with its gracefully pillared porticoes and lofty dome-covered tower. The district was colonized chiefly from Kentucky; and amongst those who went to this town from the neighbouring State was a young lawyer, who began business, and spent the remainder of his life in it—Abraham Lincoln. It was then a town of fifteen hundred inhabitants; it is now a city containing more than twenty thousand. Here Lincoln resided for thirty years. Here he brought his bride from Kentucky, and made a home with her for three and twenty years. Here, in a newspaper office, the telegram was handed to him announcing that he had been chosen President of the United States, when he quietly remarked to his friends, "There is a little woman down at our house who would like to hear this. I'll go and tell her." And here, after his tragic assassination, his remains were brought, and now rest under the memorial marble; whilst his name is engraven on the page of history, as, more than any other, associated with the liberation of three million slaves.

At this home of Abraham Lincoln, we entered on "The Springfield, Decatur, and Indianapolis Railroad," of which our friend, Mr. Hammond, has the charge. It is a hundred and seventy miles long, for about seventy of which it goes straight as an arrow; without bend, or curve, or elevation, or depression of any kind. During our journey on this line we were independent of all trains, and could choose our time and stations of call, and had an engine at our own disposal for the exclusive use of our private car.

Mr. Hammond had arranged that we should here be joined by two gentlemen, connected with the railway, whose fellowship was an additional source of enjoyment and instruction. Then, at a station by the way, another gentleman was invited to accompany us, known as Father Griffiths. He did not derive his title, however, from the Romish Church, but from Welsh Calvinistic Methodists, or Presbyterians. I had some interesting conversation with him regarding his work, and the character of the people and district around. He told me that he left his native country about forty years ago, and had dwelt in this neighbourhood ever since. It was then a part of the "forest primeval," when the noble trees began to fall before the axe, and he saw the finest timber constantly and chiefly used as firewood. He has continued all these years to act as pastor in two or three villages that here cluster together, content with the humble support which those who enjoy his ministrations can afford. He manifests his interest in the temporal prosperity of the people, as well as in their spiritual; for he brought with him specimens of bricks and tiles, which had just been manufactured on the spot, showing the capabilities of the clay; and he was anxious that Mr. Hammond should encourage the opening up of works, which he was confident would be a great success. The specimens were indeed very fine, cream coloured, hard and smooth, with a sharp edge, as if they had been enamelled. Father Griffiths expatiated on the value of this discovery, expressing his earnest desire that I would tell some of my countrymen what a profitable investment it opened up for their capital. And I hereby duly advertise the same! When he discovered that one of our company was Dr. Taylor, of New York—who was in another apartment at the time—he became quite excited, and anxious to have some conversation with him, as he had read to purpose some of his works, though not sufficiently rich to possess any. The conversation, of course, was granted, and thoroughly appreciated; and a promise was given to forward to him a presentation volume, which made the old man as happy as if a large investment had been made in the brick-works.

The soil along the line is very fertile, and in some parts, when trampled after rain, the mud formed is black as ink. But the chief crop, which we saw for long stretches, was Indian corn—food for man and beast, used in every variety of form, and, unfortunately, sometimes for the manufacture of whisky. There is a great want of enterprise, I was told, on the part of many of the farmers here, who seem content with what is produced with least labour, and spend their winters largely in idleness and drinking. Much of apparently needless wood remains, many of the fields are only partially cleared, and we saw numerous huge stumps which must be serious cumberers of the ground. The more active farmers, however, are rending these roots by gunpowder or dynamite, and the result will no doubt amply compensate for the toil and expense. We saw a wood on fire; but whether this was by accident, or to assist in making a clearance, we could not say.

The climate is genial, though, I can believe, in summer too hot for my taste; as even in the end of October there was great heat. When out at one of the villages we experienced something of a genuine tropical shower, which came on us like a pistol shot, fell in a deluge for a minute or so, then as suddenly ceased, leaving no trace of clouds from which it could have proceeded.

The towns along the line are not numerous, Decatur being the only one of consequence between the two extremes. But there are several villages, which are growing, and doubtless destined soon to rise into importance. One bears the name of *Hammond*, in honour of our friend, who has done so much to develop the resources of the district.

The railroad is in excellent condition. The rails are of the best steel, well laid, and all crossings are carefully marked by brilliantly painted wooden pailings, jutting out prominently to catch the eye of the engineer as he drives along, so that he may see them at some distance, and give due warning of his approach. Fences, too, are more attended to than is common elsewhere. These consist sometimes of wood, or of wood and wire, as with us; but in other parts they are of a more primitive character, in the shape of roots of forest trees turned on their ends. Stone dykes and hedges, so far as I saw, are things unknown in America. There is little regard to appearance, and the great quality of a fence is that it should be "horse high, bull strong, and swine proof."

The construction of this, and American railroads generally, is a much more simple matter than with us. The nature of the country, with the exception of a few mountainous or hilly districts, renders cuttings embankments, and tunnels, almost entirely unnecessary; bridges are rare—except where there are rivers or streams—as level crossings are in constant use; the expensive process of application to Senate or Congress is dispensed with, as free competition is allowed in the formation of companies, and in carrying out their work wherever they can; while ground may be easily and cheaply obtained, as proprietors and farmers are most anxious to encourage every such undertaking. Our line, as we were beginning to call it, is a new one; and, though running between two great centres of population, was not made because of any present demand, but to create and foster it. The result is already very hopeful: for cultivation, population, and even manufactures are springing up in what was, and, in many parts, still is, a comparative solitude. Great enterprise is displayed on the part of the Company, and great care taken to ensure safety. Besides the material arrangements for this purpose just noticed, moral ones also are not neglected. All servants, from the humblest stoker upwards, must be thoroughly temperate; and our friend, at the head of affairs, sets a noble example. Any of the employees found at the bar of a railway restaurant, or giving any signs of having tasted intoxicating drinks, is at once dismissed.

We rushed along this line—engine and car alone, with nothing else attached—after the fashion of John Gilpin's steed. Here a strong desire took hold of me to embrace the opportunity of riding the iron horse. All was under the control of our friend, Mr Hammond, the driver ready to show due kindness, and no strange passengers to jeer at the foolish rider seeking the saddle, or onlookers to laugh at his being helplessly, and furiously, and perhaps in terror, swept past them. So I presented my request, which was readily granted; and my friend, Mr. Bates, and I mounted bravely. I had a narrow cushion on one side of the iron shoulder, with a little window in front to break the rushing current; while the engineer occupied the other side, without any such protection. His long uncovered hair was soon streaming behind him like a comet, his broad manly face braving the terrible blast, and his eyes eagerly looking out for any danger that might arise; while, with his one hand he held control over the steam valve, which regulated our speed, and with the other he held the handle of the steam brake, by which he could very quickly bring us to a stand-still. The stoker was busy opening the little round furnace-door, and throwing in shovels-full of coals without intermission. The door was simply closed for a second, that it might be opened again to receive further supplies. The iron-horse, like the horse-leech, seemed ever to cry give, give, till I thought it must be choked. But it only roared the louder, as if to show that there was still capacity and desire for more. Along with this the incessant rattle of the wheels, and rush of the steam from the funnel, just at our ears, made the noise terrific. When any village was passed, or crossing approached, or danger of any kind apprehended, the whistle blew its loudest, and I was asked to draw the rope and ring the bell. This injunction could only be given by signs, as no voice could be heard in the awful din; and the large bell, like that of a steam-boat, though I saw it move wildly to and fro, gave forth no sound to us. The whole, however, must have combined to make our approach manifest to any beyond who had ears. All the while the engine was quivering like an aspen leaf, so that I feared, at any moment, it would be suddenly laid on its side.

Then how numerous the alarms ahead! There is a tramp!—we are sure to cut him to pieces. I pull the bell with all my might, the whistle blows several piercing blasts, and he is safe. There are surfacemen busy at work!—they may fail to notice us—renewed efforts, and all is well. Then we are on the portion of the line not without its turnings and windings—at any one of these it seems as if we might plunge into the wood, and perish in the thicket. There is a siding!—the points may be wrong, we may rush among the waggons, and smash and be smashed to pieces. Another railway comes into view, crossing ours at right angles, and on our own level. Should a train suddenly appear and meet us at that point, what a section must be made! There are constant road crossings. Some one may be on them before we are heard, and crushed beneath us! I look occasionally behind to see that nothing has happened; when I find a cart and its driver has just been arrested in time; or a litter of pigs has taken warning, and all are trotting over in safety in our wake. At one point a cow seems equally knowing, for though it has unfortunately got on the line, it has turned to the side and is pushing itself against a bank as we advance, that it might be, as far as possible, out of harm's way. A friend told me that he once saw a cow careering in full speed before a train, and between the lines, in the vain hope of outrunning it. It was impossible to stop the engine till the cow-catcher—which resembles the ram of an ironclad, and is in the front of every engine—did its work, and divided the poor creature equally in two; one portion going to the one side, and the other portion to the other side. He also told me that he knew some students who took their places on the cow-catcher, when a flock of sheep appeared suddenly ahead. The daring adventurers shut their eyes, and clenched their teeth, to meet the inevitable; but, looking up afterwards, found that all alike, both silly sheep and wise fools, had escaped.

Our ride ceased after less than an hour, when the horse required a drink, and I was not unwilling to avail myself of the opportunity to alight. I asked the driver what had been our rate. "Sixty-two miles an hour," was the reply. By this, of course, the metals of the railway, and wheels of the engine, had been well tested, and proved excellent; and so had my nerves been tried, if not with equally satisfactory results. At all events, I was satisfied with that one experiment, and have no desire to mount such a furious steed again: it seemed more like Phaëton daring to drive the fiery steeds of the sun, than John Gilpin in his perilous ride. But I think I can now understand, better than ever, the peculiarities of an American Railroad; the strain which our express engine-drivers must experience; how much we depend for our safety on their unceasing watchfulness and care; how much better it is for us to be ignorant of dangers we cannot avoid, than to be always seeking to realise those that may be before us; and how blessed it is to have One to trust who knows all the way we have to take, and has absolute control over it.

> "Keep Thou my feet; I do not ask to see
> The distant scene—one step enough for me."

It was drawing toward dusk when we reached Indianapolis. Here we had, unfortunately, to part with our friend, Mr. Hammond. He had business engagements, requiring that he should remain a day or two in the neighbourhood; while the clerical brethren had Sabbath duties to discharge, and must hasten back to New York so as to have two days of quiet and preparation. We left our private car, with all its home feeling and pleasing memories, and proceeded by the ordinary trains; not, however, without our comforts. Berths were formed for us by boards placed above, and on each side of our seats, with curtains in front; so that, though there might be upwards of thirty thus accommodated in our carriage, there was no special inconvenience.

Pittsburg was reached pretty early in the morning, and an opportunity was afforded for a kindly greeting with Mr. and Mrs. Taylor, and a brave little boy, the grandson of Dr. Taylor. In passing through the station, that I might have a look at the city, I saw a portrait of the doctor, full page size, on the broad sheet known as *Harper's Weekly*. The doctor also afterwards observed it, and making a purchase, the bookseller remarked, "That's you, sir." One of the boys, selling papers on the platform, was sharp enough to notice the likeness, and sought to make capital out of it by pointing slyly behind him, with his thumb, to the original, as he urged some one to purchase the Magazine. Another boy, appearing with the news in our car, soon made the same discovery, and came up saying, "Will you buy yourself, sir." All along the line, and for a few days in New York afterwards, this picture was conspicuous at every station; and, when Dr. Taylor himself was present, there were general signs of identification.

What we passed by night, on our previous journey, we now passed by day, and *vice versa*. But no further disclosures are needed, as we took advantage of this double experience in our descriptions of the way west. I need scarcely say here that this trip was one of uninterrupted pleasure, and, I trust, of no little personal profit. It occupied exactly ten days, and during that time we travelled 3382 miles by rail, besides taking numerous short carriage drives at different stages. We were throughout the guests of Mr. Hammond, even till our return to New York. Truly as Dr. Taylor and I remarked, he loaded us with his kindness. We have often had to notice things in America which surpassed everything of the kind at home, though we knew this would not go without question. But surely all who have followed us to any extent in this journey—though the half has not been told—will acknowledge that we cannot magnify too highly American generosity. And may I be permitted to say that, from my own people and others, I had most unexpected and substantial tokens of generosity before I left home; and that, from an unknown quarter in the old country, still further tokens were forwarded to me across the Atlantic.

CHAPTER XVI.

Washington.

A TRIP to America would be incomplete without a visit to its Capital, Washington. So, a few days before sailing for Scotland, I made out this as my final excursion.

The route was familiar from New York to Philadelphia. But after leaving the Quaker city I entered upon new ground. Our course lay along the Delaware, as it broadens into a bay, to which we occasionally come so close that we might throw a stone from the car into the water. The banks are flat, and not specially interesting; but the river is lively, where we frequently see large steamboats, or vessels under full sail, gliding along. Well cultivated farms, also, and comfortable private residences, open up, now and again, amid the clearances in the woods.

We proceed through Maryland, crossing the mouth of the Susquehanna by a bridge about a mile long, and go over, or rather through, estuaries of the Chesapeake Bay, by causeways, where it seems as if we were sailing on a finely wooded lake. Telegraph poles are ranged along, with little more than their heads above water, apparently in danger of being drenched or drowned by any little rising of the tide. Baltimore is our chief station on the way; where our crossing numerous intersecting lines and meeting trains coming and going in all directions show that we are near a great city, though only a portion of it is here seen. We will afterwards have an opportunity of looking into it, for a little, on our return.

The journey thus far had little that appeared particularly attractive, or that calls for special notice. But at length the attention is arrested by a dome of sparkling white—rising above the plain like the first view of St. Peter's from the Roman Campagna—and by a tall sharp needle-like structure piercing the sky. The one is the Capitol of Washington, the other is the Washington Monument. For miles, as we approach them, they are the only things, natural or artificial, which break the horizon. When we reach the Potomac, and cross it by a long winding bridge, a large portion of the city rises up before us; but these two objects, which at first stood out alone, now appear, by comparison with other structures, all the more enormous in their proportions, and everything else is dwarfed before them.

Arriving at the Railway Station, and anxious to improve the hour or two of daylight that still remains, I look for a cab to take me to my hotel, and through the most interesting parts of the city. In the long line waiting to be hired there is no single-horsed vehicle, and I am assured that two horses are always used, and the charge as if there had been only one. However doubtful about this last point, it may be so that horse-flesh is cheap here, and perhaps throughout America; though I would not like to give the assurance that driving is. We remain only for a minute to secure quarters at the hotel, and are soon proceeding through the Park—a fine open space that stretches down to the river.

We pause for a while at the base of the Washington Monument. It is a gigantic structure, after the style of Nelson's Monument in Glasgow; but about four times the height of the Scottish column. It is 555 feet high—the great Pyramid of Egypt is not more than 480 feet. The original intention, when the foundation of the pillar was laid, in 1814, was to raise it 600 feet; but, though it has been growing from stage to stage ever since, it was only finished some two months before I saw it—part of the builders' sheds and rubbish still unremoved—and permanently deprived of about fifty feet of the promised height.

The situation is well chosen. It stands "Even there, beside the proud Potomac's stream;" looking upon it from a point where the river is nearly two miles broad. You may ascend to the summit, and through these sharp piercing eyes—appearing from the base like those of a needle—you may gaze on the quiet waters as they steal gently to the ocean, bearing with them the memories of events of deep historical interest, and revealing scenes where the terrible conflict on behalf of slavery began. In the opposite direction you see the principal public buildings, and in fact the whole city beyond, lying beneath you. Like the National Monument in Edinburgh, this of Washington has long appeared as a broken column; only it never had anything of the picturesque character of the Acropolis of Modern Athens, and could never be taken for anything but a gigantic mistake.

We move slowly past the large Government buildings: but one of the humblest has the greatest attractions for me—the White House, or Executive Mansion—which has long been the official residence of the Presidents of America. I was somewhat surprised, not merely at its being comparatively small, but at its being painted. I thought, from pictures I had seen, and from its national importance, that it must be marble, but found it was only freestone done in oil. The stone was discovered to be porous, and required white lead to preserve it, and keep it dry. In spite of this drawback, however, the White House has a handsome appearance, and it may be well to retain it in its original simplicity, with rich historical associations that are not transferable. It was founded in 1793; Martha Washington giving her receptions in it, and several births and deaths, in the families of the Presidents, taking place in it —the last death within its walls being that of little Willie Lincoln. His mother was not very wise when there, making extravagant purchases during the war, to the indignation of the ladies of the city, who were each crying, "Let me work for my brothers, they are dying for me." Here she received the sad tidings of her husband's assassination. President Garfield, also, had only left it a few minutes, and proceeded to the railway station, when he too fell by the bullet of an assassin.

There are no military guards at the gates of the White House—in fact I cannot remember that it had gates at all—and not even the humblest officers of the law could be seen near as a protection, or to point it out as the one Palace of the chief ruler of the country. Without obstruction, or question asked, we drove up close to the doorway. A carriage is waiting there, and a gentleman steps into it. Immediately after, a lady appears; and he leaps out and gallantly hands her in. The gentleman, I am told, is the President; short and stout, with a calm open countenance, having a healthy glow; so very different from the tall thin ungainly figure of Abraham Lincoln, formerly often seen on this same spot. The lady is the wife of Mr. Cleveland, small and slender in make, with a sweet pleasing countenance. They move slowly past us, within arms' length, and I salute the great republic in them; receiving a graceful bow from the lady, and a lifting of the hat from the President. They have no outriders, or attendants of any kind, simply a two-horsed carriage with one driver; resembling in this respect, our own humble hire, though, of course, more richly ornamented. I was told afterwards that if I had handed my card he would at once have received me, and entered into conversation with me, and all the more that I was a British subject. Had I done this it might have been esteemed either a high honour or the height of conceit.

Behind the White House is Lafayette Square—a name, by the way, which seems to vie with that of Washington and Lincoln in distinguishing such scenes of recreation all over the United States. Opening up from the Square, in different directions, are the private residences of the principal citizens; or of senators and visitors who come to the capital during the Session of Congress—which extends from the month of December to the month of March. Many of these buildings are exceedingly beautiful, presenting a great variety of architecture, each house detached, sheltered in the midst of rich foliage, and, though on the line of streets, much more picturesque than the long, lofty, formal ranges at Kensington or Hyde Park.

In the evening I looked at the appearance of the city under its artificial lights; but it had then no special attractions. Many minor towns excel the capital in the means of dispelling the darkness. The breadth of its streets, requiring the two rows of lamps to stand far apart, combine, with the absence of much business and the presence of much wood, to give a sombre character to the whole.

I spent a quiet hour in visiting what is called a Cyclorama, in which one of the great battles of the Confederacy is represented in ample detail, and with considerable artistic skill. These Cycloramas are to be found in several of the principal cities throughout America, and are not merely means of recreation, but of instruction. With a friend I had looked into one at New York; on our western tour, our little company did the same at Kansas city; and I saw another largely advertised at Boston. They all deal with the same great conflict, but each with a different event in connection with it. The battle illustrated in Washington was that of Manassas, or the Second Bull Run; which had a special interest, not only as being the great turning point of the war, but as having been fought within thirty miles of where we stood, and the echo of whose guns was heard, with no small alarm, in Washington itself.

The building used here, as elsewhere, for these representations, is a kind of Colosseum, in the centre of which are the visitors, while the picture occupies a wide circle, and fills up the entire space within view. In the foreground the objects are chiefly natural, in the form of actual trees and fences, tents and huts, guns and rifles, &c., ingeniously connected with the picture, and imperceptibly blended into the scenery. A young lady was so carried away by the illusion as to express her surprise that so much of the real country could be brought within a building! I believe the work is executed with a great regard to accuracy, as it is certainly very graphic. Guide books, and a short lecture at certain hours, enable one to form a very fair idea of the battle. In attempting this, however, before the lecture and after a day's travel and a late dinner, I must confess that I stole forty winks to refresh myself in the midst of the silent scene.

These popular delineations are not the only ways by which the Americans are endeavouring to fight their battles over again. They are doing so in many of their magazines, which are largely occupied, at present, with engravings, and letterpress descriptions of the war, together with biographies of the generals and presidents of the period. Volumes, too, both historical and biographical, containing minute details and despatches of all kinds, are being issued: over which I fear many of their readers, like myself at the Cyclorama, will fall asleep. But these works will no doubt be useful in enabling some one with wisdom, patience, and literary talent, to give us a clear and connected narrative of one of the greatest conflicts of modern times.

After an early breakfast, I hastened to spend the entire forenoon at the Capitol. I approached it from Pennsylvania Avenue, the principal business street in the City, and in some respects the most striking I have seen anywhere. It has not the magnificent mansions and churches which we find in the Fifth Avenue, New York, nor has it anything like the business traffic we find in Broadway there; but it is broad, busy, and beautiful notwithstanding. It has a double line for cars in the centre, two ample carriage ways on either side, equal to most average streets, with two broad finely-paved pathways, shaded with noble trees. It is about a mile and a-half long, stretching in an unbroken line, and visible from every part. From near the one extremity, where my hotel was, I had the Capitol constantly in view, the grand object of absorbing interest at the other extremity.

This magnificent edifice is situated on an elevation, not very high, but the highest in the neighbourhood, and entirely closes in the prospect at the end of the Avenue. There it rises, in bold prominence, all the way as we advance, towering above the city like a snow-capped mount! A thin veil of mist lingers on the summit, and partially conceals it, thus furnishing scope for the imagination to magnify its height. The trees on either side of the Avenue—still green in this genial climate—hide a portion of the two shoulders or wings, and form a fine contrast to the white marble. The grand stairs, and lofty pillars and porticoes, gradually open up, and with all the more pleasing effect, as they are not approached directly in front, but slightly in profile. The whole building is 750ft. long, and 307ft. high; having full justice done to it, not only on account of the superior elevation on which it stands, but because there is ample space all around clear of buildings and beautified by gardens.

My first effort is to ascend the great Dome. It is raised high above and directly over the original one, whose foundation was laid by Washington, nearly a hundred years ago, and is in itself spacious, though insignificant compared with the vast modern structure which covers it. Walking round on the outside of the great dome, the view, in extent, and beauty, and interest, is very fine, if not grand. Green lawns, dotted with trees, shrubbery, and flowers, lie at our feet. From these the streets radiate like spokes from a wheel, and in many respects the prospect resembles that of Paris from the Arc de L'Etoile. We look from the lofty height on the proud Potomac, bounding the city to the west; and can trace its waters as far as Alexandria, where the Confederate White Flag was raised at the beginning of the Secession. The eye, also, wanders far over the undulating plains of Virginia, where the famous Manassas Junction, and other scenes connected with the war, are within view, though, unaided, we fail to detect them.

The space occupied by Washington is larger than that of Edinburgh, but the population is considerably smaller. Many of the streets have an unfinished appearance—the original plan still exceeding its execution. The great patriot, whose name the city properly bears, selected it as a site for the capital of the Republic; but, as such, he never entered it. The wisdom of his choice, however, has never been doubted. Humbolt, speaking from the most extensive observation, says, that "for site of a city, the entire globe does not hold its equal." In this we scarcely think he refers to beauty—though that might be in his mind—but to a combination of excellencies.

The Capitol, in extent and splendour without, and varied accommodation and ornamentation within, must now far surpass the most sanguine expectations of its founder; though it had to pass through the flames, during a British attack, long after his day, and can scarcely be said yet to have received its finishing touch. One of the wings, long in progress, has just been completed; but other extensions are evidently in view. I wander through halls and chambers of all kinds, used for every variety of purpose; with porches, galleries, and stairs, where I sometimes entirely lose my way. In the House of Representatives and Senate Chamber, I linger for a while, admiring their appearance as scarcely inferior to our House of Commons or House of Lords. There is one point in which they certainly excel—in providing a Ladies' Gallery in a situation of honour, where the fair ones can both see and be seen, as well as hear; and not, as with us, be cooped up behind a wire fence, like hens in a creel.

On the walls and doors of the Capitol, in the various rooms, and under the dome, are numerous representations, in bronze and plaster, in fresco and oil, of the history of the nation, from the discovery by Columbus to the last war with Britain. Amongst these pictures is a beautiful one of the *landing* of the Pilgrim Fathers; and I was reminded afterwards of a contrasted picture in our House of Commons of the *departure* of the Pilgrim Fathers; an accidental circumstance, no doubt, but suggesting opposite stand points, and the very different relation in which the two countries stood to these noble defenders of civil and religious liberty in their day.

I was struck with the absence of all representations, in the Capitol, of the recent Confederate War; and, asking an official for a reason, I was told that it would be bad taste. A pleasing touch of tenderness this for the conquered, many of whom meet within these walls, both for politics and instruction. The reconciliation between the two parties, however, is already in many ways apparent; and, as the active agents in the conflict pass away, we may well expect that all will be able equally to rejoice in the result. There is one exception, however, to the absence of memorials of the Confederate War, in a noble marble statue of Abraham Lincoln. This is conspicuous amongst many others that were presented by the various States, and which are ranged under the original dome; called, on that account, the Statue Gallery. And who can be offended at such a place of honour being granted to the true-hearted patriot whose disinterested sincerity all must acknowledge, and who became a martyr to the cause almost within the shadow of this great national building?

My attention was turned to a minor matter—and yet a feature not altogether without interest—the variety of peculiar echoes which may be heard here. Though there were many persons coming and going under the dome, a gentleman whispered to me from the side opposite to where I stood, and I heard every syllable, without requiring, as in the whispering gallery of St. Paul's, to put my ear close to the wall. He spoke again downwards, with his back turned to me, and I heard the words from an opposite quarter as coming from above. I also spoke in a whisper, addressing the floor directly at my feet, when I heard my voice coming, strong and clear, as from above. No one in the gallery seemed in the least degree conscious of the sounds produced, except the two who were experimenting.

I visited the Library in the Capitol, which, though it is by no means so large, corresponds to that in the British Museum in its relation to the people; and I was pleased to learn, that, unlike ours, it can be consulted by citizens—and I suppose by strangers too—without any introduction. In the midst of many white readers I observed a negro, black as ebony, with lofty forehead crowned by dark luxuriant hair, pouring over a huge volume, with all the thoughtfulness and conscious dignity of one who might yet find his way to the Presidential Chair. I never saw a Scotchman who seemed longer headed than this man of colour; though, in his case, some deduction might require to be made on account of the rich covering of curly wool by which his brains were protected.

I was told that even school children were allowed, and often come here to consult books; and I was charmed, in going out by the great stairs, to find a specimen. There was a negro girl, slate and bag in hand, with lively step and smiling face, seeking this royal road to learning. What a contrast, I thought, to the days, not long gone by, when to teach such an one would have been a crime, and when she might have been sold in the markets near this very spot! And what a fine pair of pictures, I imagined, might be suggested to an artist by that contrast! One might represent the slave girl, bought by some Legree, coming down the steps where she had been exposed to auction, grasped by her new and cruel master, while her face was bathed in tears. The other might represent this tidy little one, carrying proudly these symbols of free education, and tripping merrily up the great stairs of the Capitol, welcome to enjoy all the treasures of wisdom and learning which it contained. But how suddenly my pleasing picture seemed to vanish, when that little imp approached me with a sly smile, saying, "Would you give me a cent, sir?" I was beginning to lecture her on the impropriety of one so neatly dressed acting the beggar, when, with a hearty laugh, she bounded up, evidently enjoying the joke. Yet, after all, this negro girl, in such a scene of national splendour and privilege, seeking the higher education, was something worth remembering. Is it not a marvellous proof of progressive liberty and learning in America?

CHAPTER XVII.

Homeward.

O N my way from Washington to New York I broke the journey, and took a few hours at Baltimore. It was the home of some of our fellow-voyagers who sailed with us to America, and who gave me cordial invitations to visit them. I had only time, however, to see one family, which had not this association, but had friends with us in the old country. This call, besides being a social pleasure at the time, and a gratification afterwards to relatives on this side of the Atlantic—who rejoiced to have a personal link of connection with those they loved there—gave me an opportunity of seeing something of Baltimore, under the guidance of those who knew it well. Had I not obtained this glimpse, my impressions of it would have been very unfavourable; for the portion seen from the railway is by no means attractive—presenting formal rows of houses, each of the same pattern, more after the manner of an English manufacturing town than of an American city. But within I found handsome streets, formed on finely undulating ground, with excellent business premises, signs of a thriving trade, and at least one beautiful park which must be a valuable source of recreation to the busy inhabitants. There were also some superior private residences, arranged occasionally in squares; but the houses generally were built of painted brick, and require to be refreshed with a new coat every year or two. Monuments, towers and spires of churches, with various public buildings, rose conspicuous; prominent amongst these being the first Presbyterian Church and the Washington Monument. An electric railway was pointed out, with a train passing along, which I regret I had not an opportunity of testing. The busy, spacious, and finely sheltered harbour I had not time even to look at; and altogether I felt that I ought to have seen more of a city containing nearly half a million of inhabitants, and occupying a most important place in the commercial world.

It was far on in the afternoon when I left Baltimore, and late in the evening when, for the last time, I crossed the Hudson, by the Jersey Ferry, to New York. The sky was clear and blue, as it had almost constantly been during my stay in America, with the exception of some three or four days. These skies, which were beautiful by day, were solemnly grand by night. It seemed as if we were able to look through them further into the infinite, and the stars appeared with greater brightness than at home. This was, perhaps, more fully realised in the West, as at Minnesota; but even in the neighbourhood of New York, and on the bosom of its harbour, the clearness was surprising. The coal used gives forth but little smoke, and what there is must be largely lost in the great spaces of sea and river all around.

There is a weird charm in standing outside, on the little open space in front of our ferry-boat, and looking on the mysterious expanse, sparkling with innumerable and varied lights, stationary or in motion, scattered near and far. The lights of New York gradually open up like an ever-widening string of diamonds; while other steam-ferries are seen passing in different directions, their windows all aglow, like fairy-floating palaces, and casting their reflections on the dark waters in bright and broken fragments. There are barges and other vessels in our course, whose position is distinguished chiefly by lamps—on their masts or yard-arms—which look like stars of various colours and magnitudes. There is also an occasional row of vessels, drawn by conceited little tugs, which are simply floating high-pressure engines, with no more of frame work than is essential to keep them afloat, but yet possessing great power. The movements of these are made known partly by whistles or horns, some of which sounded like the cry of the laughing hyena, causing a general smile among the passengers.

A journey of three or four miles by the elevated railway—frequently overlooking sights and "sounds of revelry by night" of very doubtful character—brought me to the home of my host. The warm welcome that met me there fitly concluded this excursion to the capital, and the whole series of tours which I had made, with ever-increasing enjoyment, through a large portion of the great Continent of America.

On the eve of leaving New York, I attended two most interesting gatherings, in some respects very different in their character. The one was a social prayer meeting, held in the hall of the Broadway Tabernacle. This I felt to be specially appropriate and impressive, as, within twelve hours, I would be once more out on the Ocean. Many of the members of Broadway congregation had become familiar to me by name, or by countenance, having been introduced to them by their pastor, both privately and publicly, and having received great kindness from several of them. To part with them, therefore, was like leaving home friends; but it was pleasing to part with them by prayer.

The other meeting which I attended that evening was in honour of the French Deputies—about thirty in number—who had come to America in connection with the "Statue of Liberty Enlightening the World," which was to be inaugurated in the morning. The meeting was in the form of a banquet, held in the buildings of the Union League Club, whose numerous and spacious halls and apartments were highly decorated for the occasion, its walls covered with paintings, and its tables groaning with a rich repast. The gathering was a representative one, composed of citizens of New York in official position, and of Senators of all shades of politics, from various parts of the States. The President was expected, but he could not arrive till the morning.

For the honour of mingling with this company we were indebted to a member of the Club, who kindly sent to his friend, Dr. Taylor, and myself, cards of invitation. By introduction through these friends, and others, I don't know with how many distinguished citizens, judges, generals, and senators I shook hands. The misfortune was that most of these were previously entirely unknown to me, either by name or by fame, and there was not time now to make their acquaintance, or learn much regarding any of them.

It was gratifying to notice how widely Dr. Taylor was known, and how cordially he was received. And it was refreshing to see the overflowing geniality and good humour that prevailed among the guests, even before the feast had been tasted. I have sometimes read of the pensive spirit of the Americans; and Mr. Froude says, "The sense of sunny enjoyment is not in them." This testimony is contrary to all my experience; and a more direct contradiction of it could not be imagined than was presented by that company in the Union League Club House. I was introduced to a judge, connected with the city of New York, some of whose stories I had heard with the richest enjoyment on this side the water, and who laughed most heartily when that fact was alluded to. A certain general had the most open, smiling countenance to be found in any son of peace, and held the Scotchman's hand, long after the introduction was over, till I thought he was mistaking me for a prisoner of war, kept in the bonds of love. At the moment I did not catch the name of the warm-hearted soldier, but learned afterwards that it was General Sheridan, whose exploits are part of the history of the late war, and who is now Commander-in-Chief of the United States army.

The so-called lively Frenchmen seemed the most sedate of all. They smiled when any one was introduced to them, but soon relaxed into quiet. It was particularly so with Count Ferdinand De Lesseps, of Suez Canal fame. After he had received no end of hand-shaking, in which I had the good fortune to share, he evidently courted retirement; for, passing through one of the side rooms, we found him sitting alone on a sofa. This gave me a better opportunity of studying his features than I could have obtained by the formal introduction. His locks were of pure silver, his forehead lofty, but somewhat thrown back by the prominence of the perceptive faculties, and his face a little long, with the lines of care upon it; though his smile was pleasing. Amid the busy crowd he appeared wrapt in thought; as if the anxieties of Panama were casting a shadow, and forming furrows, which the honours he was receiving, for his success at Suez, could only partially mitigate. He confidently declares, however, that the great water-way from the West to the East—which Columbus vainly sought, and thought he had discovered nearly four hundred years ago—will be inaugurated before the close of 1889; and he expected that he himself would be on the scene of operations, by the following summer, to hasten on the work.

M. Bartholdi, the artist of the great Statue of Liberty, I only saw for a minute or so, during the process of personal introduction. His countenance was by no means so attractive as that of De Lesseps. His features were heavy; and I scarcely think he would be tempted—as is not uncommon in other cases —to make the artist his own model. His superior skill, however, in constructing in bronze, both the noble and the beautiful—whatever may be thought of his latest and most gigantic effort—is not the less real, and deservedly universally acknowledged.

Our friend conducted us through the various rooms of the magnificent building in which we were assembled, including the select library, and not excluding the large kitchen, where numerous cooks were busy in the top flat preparing, or handing out, choice dishes for the banquet. The kitchen was placed in the upper storey to prevent the savoury odours created there causing any discomfort, or impatience, to the guests below. The supplies were sent down, and empty dishes returned, by dumb waiters, that is, little elevators; whilst we were provided with the usual capacious elevator, by which we ascended and descended to the numerous storeys with the utmost speed and ease.

The banquet was begun, and the guests were gathering around tables spread with every luxury; while, amid flowers of every hue, and gorgeous tropical plants, sweet music was discoursed. But we had not time even to taste the feast, however tempted to do so, as the evening was far advanced, and we had to hasten on board the steamer, by which we were to sail with the dawn of the following morning. Dr. Taylor accompanied me to the ship, where we found his faithful partner and family looking after my young fellow-voyager with an attention that would not cease while opportunity lasted. And there, about the mid-night hour, with gratitude and regret, we parted with those who had shown us kindness and generous hospitality that were truly unbounded.

The dawn was just appearing as we moved slowly from our wharf, on Thursday, 28th of October. Our good ship was the *Britannic;* an appropriate name for one which was to take us back to our beloved British shores, as the name *Republic* had been, for that which took us out to the great Republic of the West. The motion of the vessel awoke us, and I sought the deck, as speedily as possible, to have a last look of a scene which had so charmed me on its first appearance, and had never afterwards ceased to interest. But it was not what it had been. There was nothing of the brightness of that lovely Sabbath morning on which we arrived. A drizzling rain was falling, resembling a Scotch mist, concealing much of the surroundings, and casting a cold gloom on what was visible. It was to be a gala-day, and great preparations had been made for celebrating the completion of the Statue of Liberty. Several men of war, or frigates, were drawn in line, and abundantly decorated with bunting, while colours were seen on every ship's mast, and banners on Bedloe's Island, and on the great Statue itself, which rose defiant from above the rock. All these, however, seemed more like signs of sorrow than of joy. Every flag was drooping and motionless, covered with moisture, and without a breath of wind to spread them out. After we had experienced weather of unbroken beauty—with the exception of two or three days out of the forty—it was unexpected to leave in such gloom, and especially sad for the thousands and tens of thousands who were looking forward to a grand display.

Rain continued to fall as we began to feel the swell of the ocean, and many fell sick. Fortunately I escaped this experience throughout the entire voyage. There was some improvement by the Sabbath, when, besides the usual service in the cabin, we had a service in the steerage, after the Presbyterian manner. A Welsh minister—Rev. Mr. Donne of Bangor— agreed to take part; though, being unaccustomed to preach in English, he left the sermon to me. We had the assistance of some of the cabin passengers in conducting the praise. There were a few Welshmen in the company, and Mr. Donne addressed them in their own tongue—to their evident gratification—adding a few words in English. Altogether it was a season of refreshing, in spite of the difficulties arising from the rolling of the ship. In the evening a little choir was formed in the cabin, which soon gathered around it a number of excellent singers; and sacred music greatly sweetened and sanctified the remaining hours of the Sabbath.

There were six or eight of the passengers who had previously crossed with us in the *Republic*, and with all of these we at once felt as among friends. With others, also, we gradually became more and more acquainted, finding a most genial and intelligent company. Many links of connection with mutual friends were discovered, which assisted in drawing some of us more closely together. There was on board a Duchess Dowager—connected with a Scotch estate well known in song—who also threw herself kindly into the circle. Although advanced in life, she had gone to Colorado, and was returning from a visit to a son who had considerable property in that State. I was interested in her experience, and particularly in learning from her one feature regarding the management of the property. The rent is paid by one-third of the produce, with a promise that the soil will be the farmer's so soon as he can purchase it at a price proportional to its original cost. This, I suggested, might be tried at home as one solution of the Land Question: but she thought it could not succeed in an old country! Why not?

The special feature of the voyage was the grand south-western gale through which we passed. There had been no still water from the first. But after the Sabbath the sea rose rapidly; and soon the Atlantic, putting off all restraint, showed itself in its true character, lifting itself up in its might, and surging and rolling "in fullest pride." It was fortunately fair most of the time, and we were able to be much on deck. The nights, however, were long, when, as a rule, we had to keep below. But we had many comforts there. The saloon was spacious and well ventilated, part of its roof opening above into a kind of drawing-room, where we could sit and enjoy a little of the fresh breezes coming in at the cabin stair. Our state room was most commodious, having been kindly offered us, after the first night, instead of the smaller one which we had engaged, and to which alone we were entitled. Here we had our own lobby curtained off, with a sofa inside; and while sharing our next neighbour's light, we had our own electric lamp, under which we could read as easily as during the day; and which we could make to blaze in all its soft brightness, at any hour of the night, by simply touching a knob.

Still, there were difficulties to be encountered below during the gale. It was hard at times even to keep one's berth, and yet harder to sleep. We were in a cradle rudely knocked about, and frequently on the point of being tossed out, till custom, and some little planning, overcame all hardships; and after a night or so, we slept as soundly as when everything was silent and steady. The tables in the cabin were supplied with guards, between which dishes of all kinds constantly glided from side to side, and napkin rings rolled merrily. In the midst of all, however, I never missed a meal, or ceased to enjoy one. But it was a feat to get into the saloon, and into one's place at table without stumbling: and a treat to see the stewards safely holding their trays or dishes overhead, while they themselves were waving about like inverted pendulums. Yet with all their skill, accidents did happen; and we were sorry to learn that one of the cooks fell and broke a rib.

On the deck it was amusing to see ladies

and gentlemen learning to walk; and an enjoyment, or boast, to show how steadily one could move along. Sometimes the ship's deck was as steep as a hill, and our chairs had to be tied to a fixed iron rod, otherwise they would, of their own accord, have suddenly descended, bringing us into unsafe collision with the bulwarks. A few were entirely laid low by sickness; and occasionally the main-deck was swept by a wave, to the serious inconvenience of the steerage passengers, especially of the women, who were often drenched and driven from their resting places, making sad efforts, in their sickness, to remove themselves. Some of the men, who were caught in the spray from which they had vainly sought to escape, endeavoured to laugh with those who were laughing at them. It was seldom that the upper or saloon deck was rendered in the least degree uncomfortable in this way. But there was one night when we heard, while in our berths, the rush of waters pouring down the companion-way into the saloon itself —by no means a pleasant sound in such circumstances. The carpets, however, were lifted and dried before the morning, when no trace of the disaster could be discovered.

The gale, throughout, was happily in our favour. Had it been against us, our discomfort would have been great. We could understand this as we met the *Servia*, and one or two other vessels, outward bound, facing the storm; when we saw the waves and spray dashing far up their foremasts, which must have made it impossible for any of the passengers to remain on deck, and where sudden jostlings must have been experienced, very sick-provoking to those below. These noble ships seemed to be engaged in a fierce struggle, lifting up their heads, till we could see far beneath their keels, and then, with all the strength, imparted by the might of mechanism within, plunging their sharp prows into the approaching foe, and burying them in their bosom so that the stem was entirely lost to view, while, on the wave behind, the stern rose far out of the water.

It was a new and grand experience to watch the billows from the deck, in the full majesty of their power; and, as we were rolling among them, to trace every feature, with as much carefulness and comfort as if we had been surveying them from the shore. It is fancy to speak of these as, at any time, mountains high. But they are comparatively so, and often remarkably like mountains in their form. From the trough of the sea we look up to a huge wave, just at our side, swelling, ridge over ridge, with steep ascent, and culminating in a summit which rises far above our upper deck, and entirely closes in the view. The spray, which crowns it, is like snow on an Alpine height; and over the sides the white streaks fall, or are driven by the wind, and roll down like raging cataracts. If the entire mass were to fall upon us, it would be instant destruction—and it seems sometimes as if it would; but our gallant ship lifts its head, and putting its shoulder to the work, rises steadily to the summit, from which we look down on rolling waves, like endless hills cutting the horizon all around with their rugged but lively outline.

These billows, however, as they approach near to us, are more like living monsters than mountains. Each one seems striving to overtake and destroy us; and, rushing on, fully conscious of its power, raises its head in proud defiance; but, failing in its purpose, falls with an awful roar at our side. But though they appear to look on us as foes, they are often seen to sport among themselves. Two lofty crests meet as if gently kissing each other, and then melt into one; others seem to clap their hands in joyful greeting; others, again, are like warriors in the endless mazes of the dance, with plumed helmets waving to and fro; while others come into violent collision, as if in mutual but playful conflict.

The sight from the stern is grand and striking in the extreme. There, the rise and fall of the ship is most fully felt, as we "mount up to the heaven, and go down again to the depths;" and our track behind is traced by a most remarkable appearance. A broad line of brilliant light-blue, fringed with a white foaming crest, is seen stretching from beneath far beyond, rising over, and winding round the waves in innumerable convolutions, and with unceasing motion. It seems like the great sea-serpent, wriggling and struggling after us, and writhing under the wounds inflicted by our fierce screw. Sometimes, on the top of a wave, the screw, losing its hold of the water, spins with fearful rapidity, making a kind of hissing groan, which seems to issue from the baffled monster in its agony. A few of the passengers venture to the stern to gaze on this sight; but the nerves of some fail, and they have to be led back to the mid-deck by a friendly hand.

Though not quite so striking, it is interesting to stand at the prow, immediately over the spot where the ship divides the waters. The billows here are like retreating foes, hastening to escape the conqueror. They seem in their flight to stretch their necks, and bend their heads forward, stript of much of their majesty and dignity. Every now and again one is overtaken, when our relentless prow cuts it asunder; and the dark is instantly changed into the bright blue, as the two portions, raging and foaming, fall on opposite sides of the ship.

"The storm is changed into a calm," and perfect peace reigns as we enter the Irish Channel, and proceed along the Irish coast. This continues till, about midnight, on the fifth of November, we hear the anchor dropped in the Mersey. We are welcomed by kind friends who come on board with the dawn, joined by others who meet us at the Liverpool Pier; and with the afternoon of the sixth, we are safe at home.

Thus ended our autumn holiday, extending over not more than sixty-two days, during which we had journeyed, by land and sea, fully twelve thousand miles. Well might we be filled with gratitude to Him who, throughout, had granted us His gracious protection, with so much of health and joy, instruction and social fellowship. And well may we sing the old psalm with a new meaning:—

> "The floods, O Lord, have lifted up,
>   They lifted up their voice;
> The floods have lifted up their waves,
>   And made a mighty noise.
>
> But yet the Lord, that is on high,
>   Is more of might by far
> Than noise of many waters is,
>   Or great sea-billows are."

Printed by A. Guthrie, Ardrossan.

www.ingramcontent.com/pod-product-compliance
Lightning Source LLC
Chambersburg PA
CBHW031955230426
43672CB00010B/2157